Egypt and the
Bible

Egypt and the Bible

By

PIERRE MONTET

Translated by

LESLIE R. KEYLOCK

FORTRESS PRESS

PHILADELPHIA

All Bible quotations are from *The Complete Bible: An American Translation,* by J. M. Powis Smith *et al* and Edgar J. Goodspeed, copyright 1923, 1927, 1939, and 1948 by The University of Chicago, and are used by permission of The University of Chicago Press.

First Published and Copyright 1959 by Delachaux et Niestlé

Neuchâtel, Switzerland, as

L'Égypte et la Bible

Translation © 1968 by Fortress Press

Library of Congress Catalog Card Number 68-18145

6241D68   Printed in U.S.A.   1-972

Translator's Preface

Pierre Montet, often called the "dean of Egyptologists," died on June 19, 1966, while the translation of *L'Egypte et la Bible* was still in its early stages. This memorial volume is the third of his fifteen works on ancient Egypt to be translated into English. Professor of Egyptology at the University of Strasbourg from 1919 to 1948 and at Paris' Collège de France from 1948 to 1956, Montet will be remembered primarily for his excavations of the Phoenician royal tombs at Byblos and the royal tomb of the Egyptian Pharaoh Psusennes at Tanis. At the latter site he discovered what were, until the recent discoveries at Ugarit, the most ancient alphabetical inscriptions known to man. In addition to his archaeological research he was editor of *Kêmi*, a highly respected learned journal devoted to the study of ancient Egypt. For these many accomplishments he was made a member of the French Academy in 1953.

Several major difficulties made the translation of this volume extremely taxing. First was the lack of a uniform English spelling for Egyptian proper nouns. I have somewhat arbitrarily followed the spellings adopted in James B. Pritchard's *Ancient Near Eastern Texts*, perhaps as close to "standard" spelling as at present exists. However, quotations from Egyptian literature have been translated from Montet's French text and then compared with the version in *Ancient Near Eastern Texts* as often as possible.

The sparsely-detailed footnotes in the French original were expanded from information available at the Oriental Institute library of the University of Chicago. There has been some effort to include more readily available and more recent sources in English in the footnotes and in a few cases to substitute these for the sources mentioned in the original text.

I would like to thank Mrs. Edgar H. Koch for typing the manuscripts, my wife Adrienne for reading the final draft, Dr. John A. Wilson of the University of Chicago's Oriental Institute for solutions to some bibliographical difficulties, and St. Norbert College for its support in various ways. As always, of course, responsibility for any inadequacies that remain in the translation is the translator's.

Leslie R. Keylock

St. Norbert College
January 24, 1968

Table of Contents

PART TWO: CULTURAL MATTERS

Illustrations

Plates

Line Drawings

ABBREVIATIONS

AALA   Adolf Erman, *Ägypten und ägyptisches Leben in Altertum*, rev. Hermann Ranke (Tübingen: J. C. B. Mohr [Paul Siebeck], 1923).

ANET   *Ancient Near Eastern Texts Relating to the Old Testament*, ed. James B. Pritchard (2nd ed.; Princeton: Princeton University Press, 1955).

ASAE   *Annales du Service des Antiquités de l'Egypte*

BA   *Bibliotheca Aegyptiaca* (Brussels: La Foundation Egyptologique, 1937).

BE   Pierre Montet, *Byblos et l'Egypte: quatre compagnes de fouilles à Gebeil, 1921—1924* (Paris: P. Geuthner, 1928–1929).

CP   Sir Gaston Maspéro, *Les Contes populaires de L'Egypte ancienne* (4th ed.; Paris: E. Guilmoto, 1911).

DA   Pierre Montet, *Le Drame d'Avaris: Essai sur la penétration des Sémites en Egypte* (Paris: P. Geuthner, 1941).

DBS   *Dictionnaire de la Bible: Supplément*, ed. L. Pirot, A. Robert, and Henry Cazelles (Paris: Letouzey et Ané, 1928—–).

EG   A. H. Gardiner, *Egyptian Grammar* (2nd ed.; London: G. Cumberlege, 1950).

GEA   Pierre Montet, *La Géographie de l'Egypte ancienne* (2 vols. [I. *To-mehou, la Basse-Egypte;* II. *Tochemâ, la Haute-Egypte*]; Paris: Imprimerie Nationale, 1957).

IDB   *Interpreter's Dictionary of the Bible* (4 vols.; New York and Nashville: Abingdon Press, 1962).

JEA   *Journal of Egyptian Archaeology*

L'Egypte — Etienne Drioton and Jacques Vandier, *L'Egypte* ("Collection Clio" [3rd ed.; Paris: Presses Universitaires de France, 1952]).

LRE — Henri Gauthier, *Le Livre des Rois d'Egypte* (5 vols.; Cairo: Imprimerie de l'Institut français d'archéologie orientale, 1907–1919).

NFT — Pierre Montet, *Les nouvelles fouilles de Tanis: 1929–1932* (Paris and Strasbourg: Les Belles-Lettres, 1933).

NRT — Pierre Montet, *La Nécropole royale de Tanis* (3 vols.; Paris: Typ. Jourde et Allard, 1947–1960).

RB — *Revue Biblique*

RCE — *Romans et contes égyptiens de l'époque pharaonique,* ed. and trans. Gustave Lefebvre (Paris: A. Maisonneuve, 1949).

UAA — *Urkunden des ägyptischen Altertums*

VQ — Pierre Montet, *La vie quotidienne en Egypte à l'époque des Ramsès* (Paris: Hachette, 1946).

WAS — *Wörterbuch der ägyptischen Sprache,* ed. Adolf Erman and Hermann Grapou (7 vols.; Leipzig: J. C. Hinrichs, 1926–1963).

ZAS — *Zeitschrift für ägyptische Sprache*

Introduction

Genesis 15:13 tells us that the Hebrews lived in Egypt for four centuries; Exodus 12:40 suggests that their stay may even have been a bit longer (430 years). Before Joseph had settled his brothers in the land of Goshen, Abraham had already been in touch with the Egyptian Pharaoh. Later when the children of Israel had been formed into a kingdom, they were on sometimes friendly and sometimes hostile terms with the Egyptians. Solomon married one of Pharaoh's daughters. At the same time, the enemies of both David and Solomon also received a cordial welcome at the Egyptian court. Sheshonk I seized Jerusalem; and Tirhakah, Necho, and Apries intervened in the affairs of Judah's kings.

Since we have Egyptian texts on both stone and papyrus, biblical commentators have turned to Egypt in hopes of discovering information that would add to, invalidate, or corroborate the biblical narratives. Egyptologists, too, have hoped to shed light on them. Among those who have endeavored to do so are H. Brugsch, Edouard Naville, Wilhelm Spiegelberg, Fr. Alexis Mallon, Sir Alan H. Gardiner, B. van de Walle, and others. They cannot be blamed if the results have not been as extensive as had been hoped. When the Egyptians travelled by land or sea to Palestine and Syria, they clashed with a people they designate indiscriminately as 'Aamu (possibly the Arabs) or Setyu (Asiatics). They dreaded the 'Aamu people because they crossed borders unexpectedly, ransacked isolated farms, and more than once intercepted and killed Egyptians travelling in their territory.[1] They also despised them because contrary to custom[2] they never gave the usual advance warning of an impending attack. From the XVIII dynasty on, the Shasu peoples who inhabited the land of Edom and Mt. Seir infiltrated into Egypt.[3] On several occasions they were defeated, especially by Ramses II.[4] From the reign of Thut-mose III to that of Ramses IV, a people called 'Apiru, frequently identified with both the Hebrews and the Habiru, enter the picture.[5] The trouble they caused in Palestine led Seti I to intervene. No fewer than 3,600 were transported together with other captives to Egypt where they were given agricultural tasks or even more strenuous forms of labor. Under Ramses II they worked with shepherds in the transportation of stone for the pylon at Memphis. Ramses IV sent eight hundred 'Apiru into the Rohanu Valley to haul stone to Coptos. Neither the labor nor the circumstances correspond exactly with what the pharaoh "which knew not Joseph" required of the children of Israel.

The name "Israel" occurs only once, in a single text from Mer-ne-Ptah's triumphal stele, and the passage in which it occurs is far from clear.[6]

The Bible itself does not make the task of the historian any easier. Neither the king who received Abraham, the king who placed Joseph's brothers in Goshen, the king

[1] Pierre Montet, *DA,* pp. 15-19.
[2] P. Montet, *VQ,* pp. 231-33.
[3] *UAA,* IV, 36; Henri Gauthier, *Dictionnaire des noms géographiques contenus dans les textes hiéroglyphiques* (7 vols.; Cairo: Imprimerie de l'Institut français d'archéologie orientale, 1925–1931) , V, 106.
[4] Jozef Janssen, "Les monts Se'ir (שֵׂעִיר) dans les textes égyptiens," *Biblica,* XV (1934) , 537-38; Charles Kuentz, *La bataille de Qadech* (Cairo: Imprimerie de l'Institut français d'archéologie orientale, 1928) , I, 138.
[5] Georges Posener, "Textes égyptiens," *Le problème des Habiru,* ed. J. Bottéro ("Cahiers de la Société asiatique," 12 [Paris: Imprimerie Nationale, 1954]) .
[6] Cf. *infra,* p. 24.

who was unable to stop the Exodus, nor Solomon's father-in-law is mentioned by name. The Bible knows them only as "Pharaoh," correctly transcribed from the Egyptian *Per-'aa,* "Great House," used since the days of the Old Kingdom to designate the royal palace. Beginning with the XVIII dynasty the term was applied to the king himself. Egyptology is thus forced to choose from the long list of Egyptian kings those that best correspond with the biblical evidence. For events subsequent to Solomon, the biblical data has to be compared with Assyrian and Greek as well as Egyptian texts. Inseparately linked to studies of this type is the study of places in which the Hebrews were in contact with the Egyptians. The Bible contains a rather large number of geographical names that can be identified with Egyptian sites and placed on the map. The first part of this book will thus be devoted to historical facts and geographical settings.

In the second half we shall gather all the information the Bible gives explicitly or implicitly about the customs, religion, and ethics of the ancient Egyptians. The stories of Joseph and Moses cannot be compared to the Second Book of Herodotus' *History* but since they do portray the pharaohs and the people of their court as well as the common people, it is highly important to see if they speak and act like real Egyptians and if they reveal anything about the Egypt of their day.

When the children of Israel were about to leave Egypt, their leaders warned them that they were not to be like the Egyptians among whom they had been living nor the Canaanites with whom they were to live from that time on. But when the Bible identifies Moses as one who possessed all the wisdom of Egypt and suggests that Solomon's wisdom was even greater, it invites us to investigate and see if the piety and ethics of the Hebrews have been influenced by those of the Egyptians. It would be incredible if such prolonged and repeated contacts had left no impact whatever. Since 1923 we have had an excellent source for comparison, the Wisdom of Amen-em-Opet. This work reflects ideas about God and man and about man's duties that are amazingly similar to those expressed in the book of Proverbs. If we examine these similarities we can tell what Israel owes to its former oppressors and what it may have taught them.

PART ONE

KINGS AND SITES

1

First Contacts Between Israel and Egypt

ABRAHAM IN EGYPT

The first encounter of the Hebrews with the Egyptians took place in the distant past, when a severe famine struck the land of Canaan and Abraham went down to Egypt to live (Gen. 12:10).

The Egyptians were accustomed to such visits. They knew that nomads were subject to famine. A bas-relief discovered several years ago along the causeway of Unis,[1] for example, pictures a group of extremely thin Bedouins forced to eat their own lice (see fig. 1). The Egyptians did not refuse to receive their visitors as long as they were sure that the visitors had only peaceful intentions and wanted nothing more than to rest from the stress and strain of travel in a hospitable environment — to eat, drink, water their flocks, and exchange goods. The Wall-of-the-Ruler had been constructed at the beginning of the XII dynasty to examine these emigrants and stops those bent only on plunder.[2]

---

[1]Etienne Drioton, "Une représentation de la famine sur un bas-relief égyptien de la Ve dynastie," *Bulletin de l'Institut d'Egypte*, XXV (1943), 45-54.

[2]Ermitage (Leningrad) Papyrus 1116B, 11, 66-68.

3

To the east of this wall was a military post called the Ways of Horus, that is usually located at Kantarah or somewhat to its east. Si-nuhe appeared at this post when he was given permission to return to Egypt. With his companions he waited in the shadow of the fort until the messengers sent to It-Tawy (between Memphis and the Faiyum) had returned with a permit to enter.[3]

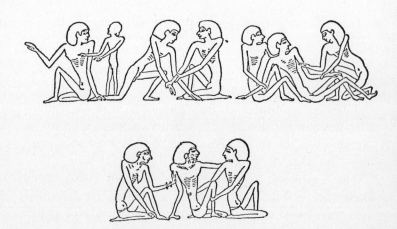

Figure 1. STARVING BEDOUINS

One of Beni Hasan's tombs furnishes a good illustration of Genesis 12:10.[4] A tribe of 37 'Aamu appeared before the governor of the Oryx-nome in Middle Egypt. They came from the waste land *ta-shew* with the hope of exchanging the black eye cosmetic *mesdemet* for grain. This time the group is not near starvation. Men, women, and children alike seem to be in good health. The women have linen coats of various colors, the men shoes and good weapons. The priest is playing the zither and the chief,

[3]Si-nuhe B, pp. 240-245; Gustave Lefebvre, *RCE,* p. 21.
[4]Percy E. Newberry, *Beni Hasan* (4 vols.; London: K. Paul, Trench, Trübner and Co., 1893–1900), II, pls. XXX-XXXI,XXXVIII.

dressed in a colorful coat, offers an ibex captured in the desert as a gift for his host (see fig. 2).

Figure 2. RECEPTION OF AN ARABIAN (*'aamw*) TRIBE IN ORYX NOME

Perhaps this painting is not exactly contemporaneous with Abraham, but it is not too remote since it comes from the time of Amen-em-het II. The story of Si-nuhe took place under Sen-Wesret I and the Wall-of-the-Ruler is attributed to Amen-em-het I: It is during this period that Abraham came into Egypt.

We do not know if the governor of Oryx found the strangers to his liking, but Abraham foresaw that Sarah's beauty would be drawn to the Pharaoh's attention and that the Pharaoh would be generous to him because of her.

Sarah's husband received from him sheep, cattle, he-asses, male and female slaves, she-asses, and camels (Gen. 12:16). The last of these gifts should catch our attention since the camel is practically unknown in ancient Egypt. This unexpected mention of camels led Erman to conclude that the Bible was mistaken.[5]

It is certainly true that the camel is not made to travel the moist slippery roads of the Nile Delta. It often sinks under its load and cannot get up again without help. "In a very short time the combined weight of a camel and its load ruins the small, so badly constructed bridges that one meets at each step."[6] On the other hand, however, it has no difficulty in the desert, and nothing prevents us from concluding that Egyptians at border posts would see camels from time to time. A small statue of a camel dating from the First Dynasty has been found at Abusir el Melek.[7]

More recently I found one at Tanis that dates from the time of the Ptolemies.[8] Although the word "camel" has not turned up in Egyptian, these two little statues vouch for the accuracy of the Abraham story.

The biblical writer does seem to be mistaken, however, when he assures us that Yahweh struck Pharaoh and his house with severe diseases because of Sarah. David will later be struck in this way for all his wickedness and particularly for having taken the wife of Uriah the Hittite. But Pharaoh is much too far above the rest of mankind, as a god and the son of a god, for anyone to discover the slightest trace in the Egyptian texts of such a punishment and prompt repentance.

[5]Adolf Erman, *Ägypten und ägyptisches Leben in Altertum* (Tübingen: J. C. B. Mohr [Paul Siebeck], 1885), p. 6. This conclusion does not occur in the second edition as revised by Hermann Ranke (1923).

[6]H. Couvidou, *Étude sur l'Egypte contemporaine* (Cairo, 1873), p. 97; quoted by L. Keimer, "Bemerkungen und Lesefrüchte zur altägyptischen Naturgeschichte," *Kêmi*, II (1929), p. 89.

[7]*Ibid.*, pp. 85-90.

[8]Information on this discovery has not been published.

THE STORY OF JOSEPH

Abraham's visit was of short duration, but Joseph's arrival in Egypt was to have lasting consequences because it was followed by the settlement of Jacob's sons in the land of Goshen. It is thus of interest to determine the date of this event as closely as possible.

Let us look first of all at the numbers which the Bible gives us. According to Exodus 12:40-41, the length of time that the Israelites lived in Egypt was four hundred and thirty years. In Genesis 15:13, Yahweh reduces this figure to four hundred years in the prediction given to Abraham. According to I Kings 6:1, the four hundred and eightieth year after the departure of the Israelites from Egypt is the fourth year of Solomon's reign. Historians give this date as 967 B.C. The tribe of Jacob would thus have arrived in Egypt in 1877 B.C., or in 1847 B.C. according to the shorter reckoning.

These dates are clearly too early. If we accepted them, Joseph would almost be the contemporary of Abraham from whom he is separated by several generations. The Septuagint gives far more acceptable figures: 215 instead of 400, 440 instead of 480. Joseph's brothers would then have arrived in 1622 B.C. The very fact that the numbers do not agree renders them suspect, but if we admit that they were established by conjecture, nothing prevents us from thinking that the Alexandrian scholars were making use of a lost source such as a complete and authentic Manetho.[9] Is there any sure way to arrive at a correct date?

The Bible, which does not mention the name of the Pharaoh or his place of residence, contains an important clue. When Joseph became second only to the king in ─

[9]These figures have been variously interpreted. Flavius Josephus in his *Antiquities of the Jews*, II. 15. 2 puts 430 years between Abraham and the Exodus, thus allowing only 215 years for the period of the sojourn in Egypt. This is obviously not long enough.

Egypt, he said to his father, "You shall live in the land of Goshen, and be near me" (Gen. 45:10). Somewhat later when the Israelites had entered Goshen, Joseph hitched his chariot and went up to meet his father Israel in Goshen (Gen. 46:28). Then he returned to tell Pharaoh the news (Gen. 47:4).

Everything takes place in a very short period of time. The Israelites have scarcely crossed the isthmus of Suez when they are in the land of Goshen. Joseph, living in the capital at Pharaoh's side, has only to make a trip in his chariot to join them, and he returns to the palace to report to his lord in the same way. As Maspéro has correctly observed,[10] a chariot is not suitable for long trips in Egypt. For long and even moderate distances a boat is the normal means of transportation. A great landowner like Ti, for example, visits his many estates in a boat. Sinuhe leaves the Ways of Horus by boat when he is invited to the palace at It-Tawy, near Lisht to the south of Cairo. For Joseph to be able to make the above-mentioned trip, the capital would have to be located not far from Goshen. We will look at the land of Goshen in Chapter 3; it will be sufficient for our present purposes to know that Goshen is in the triangle formed by Wadi Tumilat, the isthmus, and the edge of the cultivated land beginning at Pi-Soped (now called Saft el-Henneh), and extending to Tjaru near Kantarah. We can thus exclude Memphis (capital during the Old Kingdom), Neni-nesew (Ihnâsyah el-Medînah [Herakleopolis], where the kings of the First Intermediate Period ruled), It-Tawy (capital of Amen-em-het I and his successors), and even more conclusively the Faiyum and Thebes. But there is one city that meets the precise conditions we have laid down, and that is Avaris, which for more than a century was the capital of the Hyksos kings,

---

[10]Gaston Maspéro. *Etudes égyptiennes* (2 vols.; Paris: Imprimerie Nationale, 1879–1888), I, 81.

lords of all Lower Egypt and of Middle Egypt as far as Cusae.

It may perhaps be objected that the problem is irrelevant since Egyptologists do not agree on the site of Avaris.[11] The site has in fact been fixed, however. The monuments of San el-Hagar date back beyond the New Kingdom and belong neither to Tanis (founded only at the beginning of the XXI dynasty) nor to Per-Ramses. They are the remains of Avaris. Egyptian and Greek texts allow us to describe Avaris as a city dedicated for all eternity to the god Seth, the residence of the Hyksos, and a commercial city very advantageously located to the east of Bubastis.[12] The stele of the year 400 discovered at San el-Hagar by Mariette and rediscovered by the Montet mission after having been lost, confirms the fact that four hundred years before the foundation of the XIX dynasty by Ramses I, the worship of Seth had already been solidly established at San el-Hagar.[13] A recently discovered monument takes it back to the Old Kingdom.[14] The signatures of the Hyksos kings are more numerous at San el-Hagar than in any other city.[15] The Ka-mose stele discovered recently at Karnak shows that boats which came from the Syrian coast went up the Nile and docked at Karnak's pier.[16] Wen-Amon likewise in the XXI dynasty left Tanis and travelled down the Nile to Byblos.[17] This same stele also proves that Avaris was located in a region reclaimed from the marshes, called a *dja'a*. This region, called

[11]R. Weill, "The Problem of the Site of Avaris," *JEA*, XXI (1935), 10-25.

[12]P. Montet, *DA*, chaps. ii, iii, v; also the same author's *To-mehou, la Basse-Egypte, GEA*, I, 197-99.

[13]P. Montet, "La stèle de l'an 400 retrouvée," *Kêmi*, IV (1935), 191-215.

[14]P. Montet, "Ecrit à Tanis au printemps de 1956," *Revue archéologique*, I (1958), 1-20.

[15]P. Montet, *DA*, pp. 47-54, 79-80.

[16]*Comptes Rendus de l'Académie des Inscriptions et Belles Lettres* (Paris: Imprimerie Nationale, 1956), pp. 112-20.

[17]G. Lefebvre, *op. cit.*, p. 208.

Sekhet-dja'a ("Djaa Prairie") , later became *Sekhet-dja'any* ("Tanis Prairie") .

Our understanding of the kings of Avaris has increased since the discovery of the Carnavon tablet[18] and the Karnak stele. We now know that they were not the ruthless barbarians that tradition has depicted them to be. They endeavored to imitate the real pharaohs and would have loved to reunite the two parts of Egypt under their own rule. With this goal in mind they granted special advantages to the privileged few.[19] As we shall see later, however, they ruled with an iron hand.

The immense goodwill that Pharaoh showed to Joseph's brothers in permitting them to settle in the land of Goshen seems to reflect the policies of the Hyksos rulers. The native pharaohs were far less lenient. It seems likely that "since the time of Re" the 'Aamu had received permission to settle for limited periods on Egyptian soil. Later under Mer-ne-Ptah a border guard took the Shasu of Edom from the Mer-ne-Ptah fortress of Tjeku (Sile) to the marshes of Pithom and allowed them, through Pharaoh's great *ka,* to live with their flocks.[20]

From the stelae and above all from a XIII dynasty papyrus we know for certain that during the Middle Kingdom Asiatic immigrants living in Egypt were quite numerous.[21] The list given in the papyrus is particularly informative.

[18]This tablet, published in Alan H. Gardiner, "The Defeat of the Hyksos by Kamose," *JEA,* III (1916), 95-110, tells of the beginning of hostilities between the Theban Ka-mose and the Hyksos. It is the transcription of the first part of a stele erected by Ka-mose at Karnak, a few pieces of which were discovered in 1938; cf. Pierre Lacau, "Une stèle du roi 'Kamosis'," *ASAE,* XXXIX (1939) , 245-71. The completed Ka-mose stele mentioned above (n. 16) is a continuation of the broken stele. There is quite a gap between the two texts at present.

[19]Cf. Gardiner, *op. cit.,* p. 103.

[20]Papyrus Anastasi, VI, 51; cf. Alan H. Gardiner, *Late-Egyptian Miscellanies,* Vol. VII of *BA,* p. 76; Montet, *DA,* p. 145; and Gardiner, "Tuthmosis III Returns Thanks to Amūn," *JEA,* XXXIX (1953) , 7.

[21]William C. Hayes, *A Papyrus of the Late Middle Kingdom in the Brooklyn Museum* (Brooklyn Papyrus, XXXV, 1446 [Brooklyn: Brooklyn Museum, 1955]).

It was supposed to include the names of ninety-five people with their titles and occupations, but only seventy-seven have been preserved. Forty-eight of these are Asiatic, including men, women, and children. The women are employed in weaving, while the men and children are household servants, gardeners, brewers, and storekeepers. The adults have retained their Asiatic names, but the children all have Egyptian names. The public organization into whose keeping they had first been placed could sell them to private individuals, from whom they could obtain worthwhile employment. They could also be sold to other people.[22] These slaves are not former prisoners of war since the pharaohs of the Middle Kingdom did not really wage war in Palestine and Syria (whereas there were constant military expeditions under the VI and XVIII dynasties). Commercial trade between the two countries, on the other hand, is well attested. Byblos furnished Egypt with wood and boats.[23] A certain Thut-hotep settled in Megiddo and purchased oxen that he took to Egypt.[24] Asiatic laborers toiled in the turquoise mines[25] (fig. 3). This commercial exchange could very well have coincided with traffic in slaves. Those considered as undesirables by their tribesmen — Joseph, for example — and those who, like La Fontaine's dog, preferred a slave's comforts to the freedom to starve to death would be involved in traffic of this kind. That such traffic was not at all un-

[22]Georges Posener, "Les Asiatiques en Egypte sous les XIIe et XIIIe dynasties," *Syria*, XXXIV (1957), 145-163.

[23]P. Montet, *BE*, pp. 7-10.

[24]Gordon Loud, *Megiddo* (3 vols. in 2; Chicago: University of Chicago Press, 1939–1948), II, pl. 149, No. 32. The arrival of these oxen in Egypt is depicted in Thut-hotep's tomb at El-Bersheh; cf. Aylward M. Blackmann, "An Indirect Reference to Sesostris III's Syrian Campaign in the Tomb-Chapel of Dhwty-htp at El-Bersheh," *JEA*, II (1915), 13-14.

[25]A. H. Gardiner and T. Eric Peet, *The Inscriptions of Sinai* (London and Boston: Egyptian Exploration Fund, 1917); 2nd edition edited and completed by Jaroslav Černý (New York: Oxford University Press, 1952 and 1955) No. 112. Cf. Černý, "Semites in Egyptian Mining Expeditions to Sinai," *Archiv Orientální*, VII (1935), 384-89.

usual is demonstrated by the fact that Sarah had an Egyptian bond slave (Gen. 16:1).

These Asiatic slaves cannot, however, be compared to the sons of Jacob, an entire tribe that entered Egypt, settled there as a group and was permitted to multiply without check in a district that belonged exclusively to it. It

Figure 3. ASIATIC EMIGRANTS AT SINAI

was this territory that Pharaoh, sugarcoating the pill to some extent for his protégés, described as the best part of the country. Not until the XXVI dynasty was there another pharaoh who was so courteous to strangers, Amasis, who granted the Anu district in the third nome of Lower Egypt to the Greeks to get them to settle.[26]

Later we shall note that during the course of a seven-year famine, Pharaoh at Joseph's suggestion bought silver-plated objects, animals, land, houses, and finally people in exchange for food. This, too, is the act of a king of foreign extraction rather than of a native-born pharaoh.

If we acknowledge that Joseph became minister to a king in Avaris, can we become more specific and designate that king by name? The Turin Canon of Kings did contain a carefully validated list of six of these foreign kings

[26]Georges Daressy, "Stele of the Year Three of Amasis," *Receuil de travaux relatifs à la philologie et à l'archéologie égyptiennes et assyriennes,* XXII (1900), 2.

who ruled a total of 108 years but only one name, Kha-moudi, otherwise unknown, has been preserved. Manetho's abridgers are not of much help, although Josephus and Julius Africanus have retained the fact that there were six kings, and Eusebius notes that their reigns lasted 109 years. Contemporary documents mention only Khayan and three Apophises with first names of *'Aa-weser-Re, Neb-Khepesh-Re* and *'Aa-qenen-Re*. It is *'Aa-qenen-Re* who was attacked by Ka-mose.

Joseph, thirty years of age when Pharaoh promoted him (Gen. 41:46), died at 110, which was regarded by Egyptians as the ideal age. He was placed in a coffin in Egypt (Gen. 50:26) as was a man called Abdu under the second Apophis.[27] Because he wished to be buried in his homeland, he made the sons of Israel swear that they would carry his bones away with them when they left Egypt, which they did (Exod. 13:19).

The situation at the time of Joseph's death may very well not have been what it had been at the beginning of his career. Otherwise he would have been buried immediately in Canaan with his fathers, as he himself had buried Jacob's body (Gen. 50:4-7). Since this did not occur and since Joseph made the sons of Israel swear saying, "When God does indeed take note of you, you must take my bones up with you" (Gen. 50:25), his death probably occurred after 1580 B.C. when Ah-mose had expelled the Hyksos from Avaris and the whole of Egypt. Joseph's career thus coincided with the last Hyksos kings and the first pharaohs of the XVIII dynasty. The Septuagint furnishes us with figures that approximate this result. It suggests 1622 B.C., certainly close to the actual date despite the fact that it is based on inexact details.

---

[27]Georges Daressy, "Un Poignard du temps des Rois Pasteurs," *ASAE*, VII (1906), 115-120.

When Pharaoh set Joseph over all the land of Egypt, he deemed it necessary to give him an Egyptian name and a family (Gen. 41:45). Nothing could be more likely. Various stelae and the Brooklyn papyrus tell us of Asiatic slaves who took Egyptian names and disappeared into the population as a whole.[28] Under Mer-ne-Ptah a certain Ben-Ozen, originally from a country to the east of Lake Tiberias, was able like Joseph to rise to a high position.[29] He was a royal herald, fan-bearer to the right of the king, whose hands he washed. His lord gave him two names, Ramessu-em-pi-Re and Ramses-in-the-House-of-Ra-Mer-Iunu. Joseph, it will be remembered, received the name of Zaphenath Paneah (Sapnat-Paneakh) and his wife Asenath was the daughter of Poti-Phera, priest of On.

Joseph's name has been well explained by Steindorff[30] and Spiegelberg:[31] *Djepaneterefankh,* "God says he lives." Even though this exact form cannot be found in Ranke's dictionary of proper names, names of the same type are frequently encountered from the XX dynasty on, such as *DjePtahefankh,* "Ptah (or Thoth, or some other god) says that he lives."[32] One may even wonder if the word *Neter* (God), has not been intentionally substituted for the specific gods to which a native Egyptian would have referred.

Egyptologists explain Asenath's name as *Nst Nt,* "she who belongs to Neith." Many Egyptian proper names are based on the adjective *nsy,* "belonging to" (feminine *nst*), and the name of a god. Ranke has not recorded *Nst Nt,* however. I prefer therefore to compare the last half,

[28]G. Posener, "Les Asiatiques . . . ," *Syria,* XXXIV (1957), 153-56.
[29]A. Rowe, "Stelae of the Semite Ben-Aẓen," *ASAE,* XL (1940), 45-46 and pl. VIII.
[30]Georg Steindorff, "Der Name Josephs Saphenat Pa'neach: Genesis Kapitel 41, 45," *ZÄS,* XXVII (1889), 41-42.
[31]Wilhelm Spiegelberg, "Miscellen," *ZÄS,* XLII (1905), 84-85.
[32]Hermann Ranke, *Die ägyptischen Personennamen* (2 vols.; Glückstadt: J. J. Augustin, 1935, 1952), I, 123.

nath (part of Joseph's Egyptian name as well), with the Egyptian *neter* since the final *r* was no longer pronounced in the New Kingdom period. Asenath thus becomes definitively "she who belongs to God."

Two Poti-Pheras played a role in Joseph's life, the one who purchased him on his arrival in Egypt and his father-in-law, the priest of On.[33] When his name is transcribed, it becomes *Pa dy pa Re,* "the one whom Re has given." There are many names in Egyptian formed from *pa dy* ("the one given") plus the name of a god. *Pa dy Re* is attested from the XVIII dynasty on.[34] Examples with the article *pa* are rare and late, but in the Ramses inscriptions from San el-Hagar the name of the solar deity is usually preceded by the article (*Pa Re* rather than *Re*).

Thus, although the story of Joseph can be placed in the second half of the seventeenth century B.C., the Egyptian proper names belong to the New Kingdom and even to the time of the Ramses (twelfth century B.C.). This anachronism may be compared with the inadvertent reference in Genesis 47:11 to the land of Ramses, rather than Goshen, when the XIX dynasty was not yet in existence.

These facts must be kept in mind by anyone who attempts to date the final editing of the Pentateuch.

[33]More specifically, he was priest of the god Atum or one of the other gods honored at the town of On (*iwnw* in Egyptian and Heliopolis in Greek).

[34]The earliest *Padypare* known is mentioned on a stele that cannot be earlier than the XXI dynasty. Cf. A. Hamada, "Stela of Putiphar," *ASAE,* XXXIX ((1939), 272-77.

2

Moses and the Exodus

RAMSES II

The time has come to identify the Pharaoh who "knew not Joseph" (Exod. 1:8) and placed forced labor foremen over the sons of Israel (Exod. 1:11).

Let us first of all consider the numbers which the Bible gives. The Septuagint translation estimates the time interval between the building of Solomon's Temple (967 B.C.) and the Exodus at 440 years, thus giving the date 1407 B.C. which coincides with the beginning of Amen-hotep III's reign. According to the Hebrew version, which puts the Exodus forty years earlier, the event would have taken place during the reign of Amen-hotep II and the Pharaoh who oppressed the Israelites would be none other than Thut-mose III.

Each of these views has its supporters.[1] Two arguments have been brought forward. Several scholars con-

[1]E. Lefebvre, "La mention des Hébreux par les Egyptiens s'accorde-t-elle avec la date de l'Exode?" in *Oeuvres diverses*, II, Vol. XXXV in *Bibliothèque égyptologique* (Paris: Ernest Leroux), 1912, 471-77; Alexis Mallon, "Les Hébreux en Egypte" *Orientalia*, No. 3 (Rome: Pontificio Instituto Biblico, 1921), pp. 178-81; Sir Charles Marston, *The Bible is True: The Lessons of the 1925–1934 Excavations in Bible Lands Summarized and Explained* (London: Eyre and Spottiswoode, 1934), pp. 170-80. Jozef Janssen, "Les monts Se'ir (שֵׂעִיר) dans les textes égyptiens," *Biblica*, XV (1934), 538; B. van de Walle, "Hyksos," in *DBS*, Vol. IV, col. 165.

clude that since the sons of Israel were allowed to settle in Goshen by the Hyksos kings, their departure must have followed quite closely the recapture of Avaris in the first half of the sixteenth century B.C.[2] This reasoning does not seem valid to me because the question can be raised whether the sons of Israel could not have been forgotten or tolerated by the conquerors. They had not come as conquerors with weapons in their hands but rather as beggars asking for food. They were harmless and could even have been useful. Had they been dangerous, Ah-mose the conqueror of Avaris would have settled with them on the spot.

The second argument is based on excavations of Jericho, one of the three cities which, with Hazor and Ai, were captured and set on fire by Joshua more than forty years after the flight from Egypt. Garstang, who excavated Jericho with genuine persistence, has distinguished (as have other archaeologists for Troy and Mycenae) the remains of several cities, one superimposed on the other.[3] Jericho IV, whose double wall was discovered in a fallen state and whose palace and houses show traces of fire, has yielded potsherds, weapons, pearls, and scarabs, all of which date before 1400 B.C. Scholars have noted, on the other hand, the almost complete absence of Mycenaean potsherds.

The attempt to date a historical event such as the capture of Jericho by means of archaeological artifacts is not to be condemned since excavations have produced no inscription even remotely close to the event; but scarabs and

---

[2] A. H. Gardiner, "Tanis and Pi-Ramesse, a Retraction," *JEA*, XIX (1933), 127; René Dussaud, "Quelques précisions touchant les Hyksos," *Revue de l'histoire des religions*, CIX (1934), 127.

[3] John Garstang, "Jericho, City and Necropolis," *Annals of Archaeology and Anthropology* (Liverpool), XIX (1932), 3-22, 35-54; XX (1933), 3-42; XXI (1934), 99-148; XXII (1935), 143-84; XXIII (1936), 67-100; summarized by Georges A. Barrois in his *Manuel d'archéologie biblique* (2 vols.; Paris: A. Picard, 1939–1953), I, 171-83.

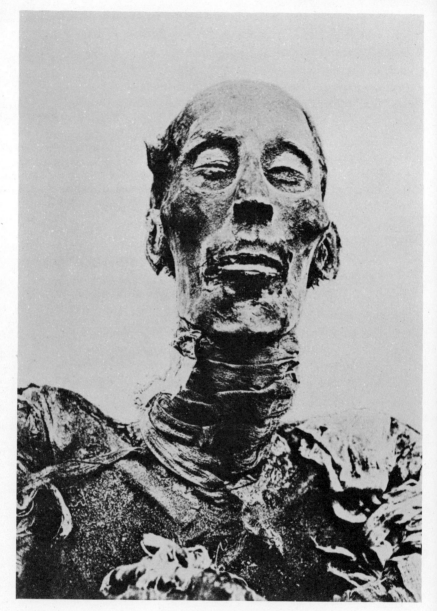

Plate I. Mummy of Ramses II

potsherds are not very dependable witnesses. Scarabs move about a great deal and one never can be sure if they come from the time of the king whose name they bear. Scarabs with the name of Thut-mose III were made down to the Ptolemaic period. Moreover, the Jericho excavations have produced very few scarabs; several are attributable to the Hyksos, one to Queen Hat-shepsut, two to Thut-mose III, and one to Amen-hotep III. The absence of scarabs previous to this period thus proves absolutely nothing. In fact, the book of Exodus if used with care, contains the data which allow us to resolve the chronological problem.

The first fact concerns the long life of the oppressive Pharaoh. He had already been reigning for some time, and persecution had begun when Moses was born. Moses waited until he was eighty (Exod. 7:7), and the persecuting king had died before speaking to Pharaoh. The sons of Israel who had endured their fate in silence now groaned about their bondage. Who then is the Pharaoh who, after a long and glorious reign, was followed by a much weaker king under whom what had seemed impossible up to that point now seemed to be within reach? Only one king during the whole New Kingdom fits the requirements — Ramses II. He ruled for 67 years and imposed on his opponents a peace which was unbroken during the second half of his reign (pl. I). Mer-ne-Ptah was not so fortunate, and the Libyan invasion which came within a hair's breadth of destroying Egypt in the year V was an unexpected opportunity for the sons of Israel.[4]

The second indication concerns the cities in which the sons of Israel labored (Exod. 1:11), Pithom and Ramses, that the Chronicler calls store-cities for Pharaoh. These cities will be discussed more fully in Chapter 4; at this

[4]Thut-mose III reigned 54 years (including Hat-shepsut's regency), but his son, Amen-hotep II, the sportsman-king par excellence, was no man to tremble before Moses and Aaron.

point I merely wish to point out the error of those who maintain that Ramses II adorned and enlarged Pithom and Ramses but that he did not build them.[5]

In the Middle Kingdom there were ancient and prosperous cities throughout the eastern Delta in which the pharaohs had built, at great expense, temples of good, sound stone: Avaris, Pi-Soped, Pithom, Ime. These cities were totally neglected by the kings of the XVIII dynasty. Amen-hotep III worked at Athribis because his main minister, Amen-hotep the son of Hapu, had been born there. Other kings had works built at Bast and Tjaru because these towns were situated on the main road from Egypt to Syria, but everywhere else the same observation can be made. The Old and Middle Kingdoms and even the Second Intermediate Period have left remains that are often important, but the XVIII dynasty has not. Monuments were constructed everywhere under Ramses II — at San el-Hagar, Tell el-Maskhuteh, Bast, Horbeit, and along the Canal of the Pharaohs.[6]

It is not hard to explain this difference in practice. Originating in Thebes, the XVIII dynasty pharaohs were not inclined to pour out their bounty on towns that had been sullied by the presence of the Hyksos and that had gotten along with the foreigners, vile slaves that had revolted against their Egyptian overlords. But the XIX dynasty was quite different from its predecessor. Descended from an ancient family from whom the great priests of Seth (disliked by the Thebans) including Prince Seti, the future Seti I, were recruited, this dynasty (which after the death of Hor-em-heb around 1320 or 1315 took the place of a completely exhausted family line) at first wanted to

---

[5]Adolphe Lods, *Israel From its Beginnings to the Middle of the Eighth Century* (New York: Alfred A. Knopf, 1932), p. 185.
[6]P. Montet, *DA,* chap. iv.

rally the devotees of Osiris and Amon. Ramses II, however, deciding that the future was his, had other plans. No
sooner had mourning for his father ceased than he went
in his royal boat, escorted by a whole fleet, to found a
capital that was to receive his name in the eastern Delta
region.[7] He did not like the climate of Thebes and wanted
to place as great a distance as possible between his residence and that of the priesthood of Amon, still inclined
to dictate to Egypt's kings. This plan forced him not only
to build a capital but also to revive a desolate region and
to improve his communications with the great cities of
On and Memphis, the whole of Upper Egypt, and also the
whole Delta and the countries to the east.

In this way Ramses II was led to put into practice a
new policy regarding Jacob's descendants who had settled
in the land of Goshen and even in the surrounding regions. Successful wars had given him prisoners who worked
in the quarries and pulled stone blocks in the stone-yards,
but he also needed to think about walls and storehouses
made of rough bricks, and to manufacture these materials
in great quantity and at a high speed. It is understandable
that Ramses would not want to impose this task on the
Egyptians[8] and that he would prefer to give it to foreigners
who had been welcomed when in need and who had become so numerous that in the event of war they could go
over to the side of the enemy (Exod. 1:10).

Thirdly, we will apply to Ramses II the observation we
made about the king who promoted Joseph. Once settled
at Avaris, this king had the sons of Israel as close neighbors. Pharaoh's court in the days of Moses was clearly

---

[7]See the dedicatory inscription of Abydos, line 29, in *ZAS*, XLVIII
(1910), 42-66.
[8]Diodorus *Bibliotheca historica* i. 56 notes that Sesostris did not use
Egyptians in his construction work.

in contact with the sons of Israel, since Pharaoh's daughter, as she came down to bathe with her female companions, noticed little Moses' basket. When he had grown up, Moses spoke with Pharaoh almost at will without going far from his people. Then, too, as soon as he was told of the Exodus, Pharaoh set out in pursuit of the fugitives. The many texts which relate to the residence of Ramses II in the Delta (Per-Ramses, to give it its Egyptian name) prove not only that Ramses II made many long stays there (pl. II), but also that his first successors Mer-ne-Ptah and Seti-Mer-ne-Ptah followed his example.[9] Favor for this residence reached a low ebb under Ramses III; nevertheless he had works built and celebrated his jubilee here. Many times we run across the name of Ramses VI here,[10] but we hear nothing about it from then until the War of the Unclean.[11]

This observation completely eliminates the kings of the XVIII dynasty who all lived in Upper Egypt, some at Thebes and others at Akhetaton (Tell el-Amarna). Memphis, Bubastis, and Tjaru undoubtedly were visited by these kings during their wars in Syria or on their return laden with enemy spoils, but those visits were never of long duration. The episode of Pharaoh's daughter cannot be placed during this period, nor can we imagine Moses stopping the king's procession to present him with the demands of his people.

[9]These have been gathered, translated, and annotated by A. H. Gardiner, "The Delta Residence of the Ramessides," *JEA*, V (1918), 127, 179, 242. Eliminate number 17 and add the Beisan stele (A. H. Gardiner, "The Geography of the Exodus," *JEA*, X [1924], 93). Cf. also Pierre Montet, *DA*, pp. 118-43.

[10]See a granite stone reused at Tanis in the pavement of the main thoroughfare and a statue from the northern temple. This information has not been published elsewhere.

[11]P. Montet, *DA*, chap. v.

Plate II. RAMSES II PROTECTED BY HURUN OF RAMSES, FROM THE TANIS COLLECTION

MER-NE-PTAH

During the long period of persecution the Bible mentions only one change in rule (Exod. 2:23). It follows from what we have established that it was under Mer-ne-Ptah, son and successor of Ramses II, that the conflict between Israel and Pharaoh became increasingly serious and resulted in the Exodus.

There is one difficulty, however. Moses was eighty years old when he returned from the desert to speak to Pharaoh (Exod. 7:7).[12] Let us accept this statement for the moment. We know that Ramses II ruled 67 years.[13] Dr. Fouquet's study of his mummy at the time of its discovery points to an age of ninety years (pl. I)[14] He was thus twenty-three when he ascended the throne. His daughter when she adopted Moses was old enough to take a walk with her friends and to make a decision. Thus it is difficult to place Moses' birth prior to the tenth year of his reign. Persecution had already lasted some time. Moses' intervention would thus have occurred some twenty years after the death of Ramses II, not during the reign of Mer-ne-Ptah (which only lasted ten years) but during that of Si-Ptah or even Seti II. It may be, however, that all the figures have been rounded off somewhat. For this problem it is above all the Mer-ne-Ptah Stele, called the "Israel Stele" and discovered by W. M. F. Petrie in the temple of Mer-ne-Ptah at Thebes, which must be considered.[15]

[12]Moses' age at this decisive moment is corroborated by the author of Acts (7:23-30); Moses, who was forty when he fled after the murder of the Egyptian, returned forty years later.

[13]H. Gauthier, *LRE,* III, 49.

[14]G. Maspéro, *Les momies royales de Deir el-Bahari,* Vol. I in *Mémoires de la Mission Archéologique Française du Caire* (Paris: Ernest Leroux, 1884), p. 774.

[15]Cairo 34025. Cf. W. M. F. Petrie, *Six Temples at Thebes* (London: B. Quaritch, 1897), pls. XIII–XIV; Pierre Lacau, *Stèles du Nouvel Empire* ("Catalogue général des antiquités égyptiennes du Musée de Caire" [Cairo: Imprimerie de l'Institut français d'archéologie orientale, 1909——]), I, 52 ff. with its Bibliography; and James B. Pritchard, *ANET,* p. 378, for the translated quote.

In the last lines of this long panegyric we read the following:

> The princes are prostrate, saying: "Mercy!"
> Not one raises his head among the Nine Bows.[16]
> Desolation is for Tehenu;[17] Hatti is pacified;
> Plundered is the Canaan with every evil;
> Carried off is Ashkelon; seized upon is Gezer
> Yanoam is made as that which does not exist;[18]
> Israel is laid waste; his seed[19] is not.
> Hurru is become a widow[20] for Egypt.

The interpretation of this text is far from clear. For the majority of authors Mer-ne-Ptah actually conducted or sent an expedition into Palestine in order to complete his victory over the Libyans.[21] But by this hypothesis how can mention of Israel be explained? Scholars who place the Exodus in the XVIII dynasty think that during the Palestinian campaign Egyptian forces met and defeated Hebrew tribes that attempted to enter Canaan from Kadesh-barnea.[22] Those who date the Exodus at the time of Mer-ne-Ptah suppose that other Israelites led a nomadic existence on the other side of the Suez isthmus.[23] A third

[16]The Nine Bows are the peoples or lands which owe obedience and military service to Pharaoh, i.e., Upper and Lower Egypt and the seven surrounding lands including Tehenu.

[17]One of the Libyan peoples.

[18]A frequent cliche in triumphal stelae.

[19]The word *prt* has two meanings in Egyptian: "grain for sowing" and "posterity"; cf. A. Erman and H. Grapow, *WAS*, I, 550. W. Spiegelberg, "Der Siegeshymnus der Merenptah," *ZÄS*, XXXIV (1896), 1-25, translates it "cereals" and concludes that the sons of Israel plunging into the desert were to perish in a short time. Cf. also A. Erman, *The Literature of the Ancient Egyptians*, trans. A. M. Blackman (London: Methuen and Co., 1927), pp. 274-78.

[20]A play on the words *Ḫaru/Kharu* "Hurrian" and *ḫaret*, "widow."

[21]Etienne Drioton and Jacques Vandier, *L'Egypte*, Vol. II of *Les peuples de l'Orient mediterranéen* ("Collection Clio" [4th ed.; Paris: Presses Universitaires de Paris, 1962]), p. 431.

[22]A. Lods, *op. cit.*, pp. 214-15.

[23]E. Drioton, "La date de l'Exode," *Revue d'histoire et de philosophie religieuses*, I (1955), 45; B. van de Walle, "Inscriptions égyptiennes," in *DBS*, Vol. IV, cols. 445-46.

hypothesis would consist of maintaining that the Israelites who were so maltreated were precisely those who lived in Goshen who had the audacity to revolt against Pharaoh.[24]

These hypotheses have in common the assumption that the Palestine campaign really took place. It is precisely this point that has not been established. The question of whether Thut-mose III actually conquered Syria from one end to the other and reached the Euphrates, whether Seti I severely punished the peoples of central Palestine who revolted, or whether Ramses II clashed at Kadesh with a gigantic coalition of forces, has not been settled. The texts that relate these events record the army's departure, its advance, the decisive encounters, and the triumphal return. But there is nothing of the kind here. A simple statement of the facts is enough. The Hatti, faithful to their treaties, remained at peace. The ethnic groups which had undoubtely displayed warlike designs and were ready to share the spoils were reluctant to move when they heard of the defeat of the Libyans.

Egypt had in fact had a narrow escape. The Libyan army that came from the west evidently had Memphis as its goal. It could have sailed up the Canopic branch of the Nile and attacked the old capital from the north or the west. This was what the Egyptians expected. But the Libyan leader had another idea. The great Mer-ne-Ptah Stele at Karnak shows the Libyans pitching their tents in front of Per-Berset and encamped on the banks of the Itj canal.[25] As Gardiner has demonstrated,[26] Per-Berset is Bubastis. The Itj canal, repeatedly mentioned in Egyptian texts, irrigated On, and possibly Bubastis, and flowed into

---

[24]*Ibid.*, p. 446.

[25]Cf. W. Max Müller, *Egyptological Researches* (3 vols.; Washington: Carnegie Institute, 1906–1920), I, pls. XVII-XXXII. The English translation of the passage will be found in Alan H. Gardiner, "The Delta Residence of the Ramessides," *JEA,* V (1918), 258.

[26]Gardiner, JEA, V, pp. 258-59.

a lake in Soped Nome.[27] So one corps of the invading army by heading east deceived the Egyptians and cut off Memphis, On, and of course all Upper Egypt from all locations located north of Bubastis. The enemy undoubtedly depended on a general uprising of the peoples living in the land of Canaan and southern Palestine, not to mention the sons of Israel who endured their subjection to hard labor so poorly. The fears that the Bible attributes to Pharaoh in Exodus 1:9-10 were thus confirmed:

> "See, the Israelite people have become too numerous and too strong for us; come, let us take precautions against them lest they become so numerous that in the case of a war they should join forces with our enemies and fight against us, and so escape from the land."

Mer-ne-Ptah's victory against the Libyans (in a place whose location is uncertain and for which indisputable textual evidence is lacking[28]) forced the invading army to withdraw and nipped in the bud the warlike ambitions of Egypt's immediate neighbors whose only thought now was to submit to Egypt.

If we have interpreted the Mer-ne-Ptah Stele correctly, it becomes clear that the sons of Israel were still in Egypt in the fifth year of this king's rule. They were undoubtedly not there much longer than that. Moses and Aaron figured that after a victory obtained in the nick of time, their oppressors no longer had the strength they once had and that they could no longer seriously resist their departure.

Joseph's brothers, we have noted, settled in Egypt around 1620 B.C. Moses and his people left in 1228. The duration of the stay of the sons of Israel in Egypt was therefore around 390 years, perhaps a little less, but hardly

[27]P. Montet, *GEA*, I, pp. 169, 211.
[28]H. Gauthier, *Dictionnaire des noms géographiques contenus dans les textes hierglyphiques* (7 vols.; Cairo: Imprimerie de l'Institut français d'archéologie orientale, 1925-1931), II, 58-59.

more. Our estimate is thus very close to the 400 years given in the prediction to Abraham (Gen. 15:13).

The 400 figure brings to mind a significant document, the Stele of the Year 400 found at San el-Hagar by Mariette, then lost until its rediscovery by our Tanis mission.[29] The era beginning in the year 400 was inaugurated by a king named Seth-apehti Nubti, founder of a short-lived kingdom just prior to the Hyksos invasion; it came to a close around 1318 B.C. when Ramses I founded the so-called Menophres era at the same time as the XIX dynasty.[30] It probably has nothing to do with the stay of the Israelites. It did take place, however, about the time when the Israelites were in the land of Goshen and thus confirms the length of their stay in that land.

Mer-ne-Ptah died after ruling ten years. He had a tomb built in the Valley of the Kings which was desecrated during the troubles which occurred at the end of the XX dynasty. His mummy was then conveyed to a chamber in the tomb of Amen-hotep II which had been converted into a royal hideaway (pl. III). It was recovered by V. Loret in 1898.[31]

At the same time Mer-ne-Ptah had a cenotaph in the *ḥer* cemetery of Ramses.[32] This *ḥer* is only known from texts, but Mer-ne-Ptah's sarcophagus, taken over by Psusennes and discovered by our Tanis mission in Psusennes' tomb, is a detached part of it. Mer-ne-Ptah's cartouches have been erased and replaced by those of Psusennes but the work was done carelessly. Several fragments of the original name and the whole name on a belt buckle

[29]P. Montet, "Le Stèle de l'an 400 retrouvée," *Kêmi*, IV (1935), 191-215.
[30]P. Montet, *DA*, pp. 111-12.
[31]Cf. Sir G. Elliot Smith, *The Royal Mummies* (Cairo: Imprimerie de l'Institut français d'archéologie orientale, 1912), pls. XLVI-XLIX.
[32]Ramses' *ḥer*, which appears in Papyrus Anastasi, VIII, 9-10 in *JEA*, V (1918), 197, was located at the edge of the Ra Stream, the Tanitic branch of the Nile in its lower course. Cf. P. Montet, *GEA*, I, pp. 195, 200-201.

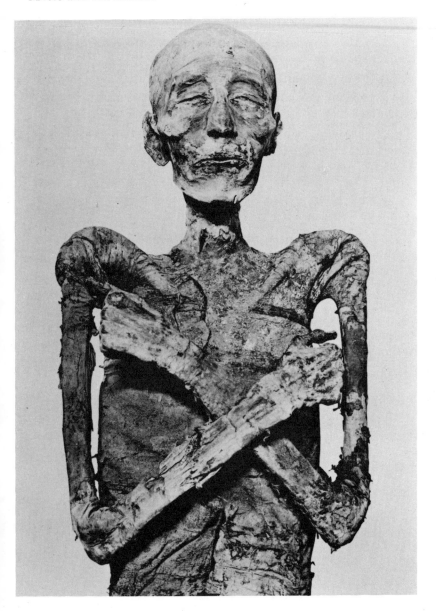

Plate III. MUMMY OF MER-NE-PTAH

establish the truth. The person stretched out on the lid of the sarcophagus thus offers us a picture, probably the best we possess, of the pharaoh of the Exodus (pl. IV).[33] It can be compared with Mer-ne-Ptah's mummy. The expression, majestic and paternal at the same time, agrees well with this king's character as presented in the book of Exodus, hard and imperious but at the same time extremely sensitive.

MOSES' NAME

Moses' name, *Mosheh,* is generally considered to be of Egyptian origin (Exod. 2:10).[34] The child, so the story goes, became a son to the princess who had saved him. No doubt there was a legal adoption. Pharaoh's daughter would take the place of the parents in naming the child. She could have meant nothing else by the well-known sentence, "For I drew him out of the water" (Exod. 2:10).

Josephus and many others after him have believed that these simple words contained the explanation of the name.[35] The Egyptians, he says, call water $\mu\tilde{\omega}$ and those saved from it, $\dot{\upsilon}\sigma\eta\varsigma$. Philo also says water is called $\mu\tilde{\omega}\upsilon$,[36] but he slides over the last part of the name. Whether it be $\sigma\eta\varsigma$ or $\dot{\upsilon}\sigma\eta\varsigma$, it can be related to the word *hsy,* "praised," which is said of drowned persons who have been fished out, later to be buried in a sepulchre. The idea of immortality through drowning became popular in the last centuries before Christ.[37]

[33]P. Montet, *Les constructions et le tombeau de Psousennes à Tanis,* Vol. II of *La Nécropole royale de Tanis* (3 vols.; Paris: Typ. Jourde et Allard, 1947–1960), pl. LXXVII.

[34]Alan H. Gardiner, "The Egyptian Origin of Some English Personal Names," *Journal of the American Oriental Society,* LVI (1936), 192-94.

[35]Josephus *Antiquities of the Jews* II. 128; *Against Apion* I. 286.

[36]Philo *On the Life of Moses* I. 4.

[37]Jaroslav Černý, "Greek Etymology of the Name of Moses," *ASAE,* LI (1951), 349-54.

Plate IV. PORTRAIT OF MER-NE-PTAH ON HIS SARCOPHAGUS, STOLEN BY PSUSENNES

Pharaoh's daughter certainly did not think about all that. She gave the child the first name that came to her head, *Mose,* which forms the second half of such names as Thut-mose, Iah-mose, and Ra-mose. These names mean "such and such a god is born" and were given to children born on the anniversary of the god's birth. Had the princess forgotten what god had been born on the day she found Moses? In Egypt the god's name is frequently understood and thus *Mesw* or *Mesy* often occurs alone.[38]

Could not one of them possibly be the leader of the sons of Israel? Two Ramesside papyri that date approximately from the reign of Seti II[39] mention a certain Moses, a terrible and mysterious figure who can punish the incompetent civil servant and even remove a vizier from office. Above the vizier, as Černý notes,[40] there was only the pharaoh. One can therefore quite legitimately think of one of the last kings of the XIX dynasty, Amen-mose, whose name would have been shortened to Mose, just as Ramessu was familiarly known as Sessu. It may also be wondered whether an unknown pharaoh may not have had at his side a favorite named Mose before whom even the most powerful men trembled. To conclude from this, however, that the favorite was Moses is a leap that I for one do not wish to make.

Some other biblical characters have Egyptian names. Phinehas, the son of Eleazar (Exod. 6:25; Num. 25:7) has a name that closely resembles *Panehsy,* "the Negro."[41] A Panehsy was head of the treasury under Amen-hotep III; another, vizier under Mer-ne-Ptah; and a third the royal son of Kush under Ramses XI. Susannah, too, is formed

[38]Hermann Ranke, *Die ägyptischen Personennamen* (2 vols.; Glückstadt: J. J. Augustin, 1935 and 1952) , II, 227.

[39]Papyrus Anastasi, I, 18, 2 and Papyrus Salt 124.

[40]Jaroslav Černý, "Papyrus Salt 124 (Brit. Mus. 10055)," *JEA,* XV (1929), 255.

[41]Gardiner, "The Egyptian Origin . . . ," *Journal of the American Oriental Society,* LVI (1936) , 192-94.

Figure 4. PHILISTINE PRISONERS OF RAMSES II

from *shoshan,* "lily," a word borrowed from the Egyptian *sšn,* "the white water-lily."[42] On the other hand the attempt to find an Egyptian origin for the name of Moses' sister, Miriam (Exod. 15:20, Num. 19:1; 20:1) from *mryt,* the feminine participle of *mry,* "to love," must be abandoned. The transcription *mry 'Imn,* "beloved of Amon," which is *Maï-amama* in Babylonian and Μιαμουν in Greek proves that the *r* had been assimilated.

After the Exodus, relations between Israel and Egypt were interrupted for a long time; or at least they have not left behind any textual evidence. However, those great enemies of Israel, the Philistines, were soon going to confront the Egyptians and share in the savage attack of the

[42]*Ibid.,* pp. 189-90.

33

Sea Peoples. They would suffer great losses and leave many of their number in the hands of Ramses II's soldiers (fig. 4). Nevertheless the Egyptians would not be able to prevent the Philistines from occupying the coastal cities of Canaan from which it would be possible for them to harass Egyptian merchants going to Byblos to purchase wood.

The Philistines were a jolly people who dressed like the Canaanites and, what is more unusual, wore a loincloth decorated with tassels as did Ramses' god, Seth. They protected their heads with a helmet surmounted by a crownpiece covered with feathers. The Bible and Egyptian documents both suggest that the Philistines quickly adopted the Canaanitic way of life.

3

From David to Jeremiah

After the Egyptians decided not to pursue them, the sons of Israel travelled in the desert, crossed the Jordan, conquered Palestine, and founded a kingdom without the slightest opposition from their former oppressors.

Mer-ne-Ptah in the second half of his reign appears to have been idle. The last years of the dynasty were quiet. The same cannot be said for the reign of Ramses III (1198-1166), who had trouble combatting two Libyan invasions and the attack of the Sea Peoples. During the course of a Syrian campaign he seized several strongholds but these successes were ephemeral.[1] After him Egyptians appeared from time to time in Syria and Palestine but they ceased to be dreaded rulers.[2]

It is in the Bible that we find the first piece of evidence concerning the kingdom of Israel and Egypt. One of Solomon's enemies, Hadad, who had escaped the massacre of the Edomites went down to Egypt with his servants and some men from Paran (I Kings 11:14ff.). Pharaoh gave him a favorable welcome and the sister of his own wife, Tahpenes the queen, in marriage. The son born of this marriage was raised in the court. When Hadad learned

[1]On Ramses III in Palestine, cf. B. van de Walle, "Inscriptions égyptiennes," in *DBS*, Vol. IV, cols. 448-49.
[2]Ramses IX's envoys to Byblos were kept there against their will; cf. Gustave Lefebvre, *RCE*, p. 217.

of David's death, he asked for permission to go back to his homeland and rule over Edom. Pharaoh is mentioned only by his title, but we do have a chronological landmark, since David died in 980 B.C., after ruling about forty years. This story thus took place during the second half of the XXI dynasty which lasted from 1085 B.C. to 950 B.C. Founded before the accession of Saul, it came to a close at the time of Solomon's death.

Following the War of the Unclean,[3] which had caused a great deal of destruction and misery, the XXI dynasty faced a difficult situation. Smendes,[4] its founder, established order once again, constructed a new residence, Tanis, on the ruins of Avaris and Per-Ramses and despite a number of rebuffs renewed relations with Byblos. His successor Psusennes completed the reconstruction of Tanis.[5] His long reign does not seem to have been enriched by many events of significance.[6] He did, however, style himself a captor of cities.[7] He also practiced the art of political marriage, which had been the custom for the kings of the XVIII dynasty and for Ramses II, by marrying an Assyrian princess, Napalta, daughter of the vizier Ibishshi-ilu.[8]

The fifth king in this dynasty, Siamon, was probably a contemporary of David. The records that we have of this king are chiefly of his buildings and foundations in the land of Kêmi.[9] However a fragment of a bas-relief I dis-

---

[3]P. Montet, *DA*, chap. V.

[4]Smendes was a descendant of Ramses who had abandonded the supporters of Seth for the side of Amon. Cf. P. Montet, *Les constructions et le tombeau de Psousennès à Tanis*, Vol. II of *NRT*, pp. 178-79.

[5]*Ibid.*, pp. 14-27.

[6]*Ibid.*, pp. 9-14.

[7]*Ibid.*, p. 75, No. 714.

[8]*Ibid.*, pp. 139-43. (Trans.: *In Eternal Egypt* (London: Weidenfeld and Nicolson, 1964), p. 49, Montet says *Psammetichus* was the pharaoh who married Napalta.)

[9]H. Gauthier, *LRE*, III, 298.

covered at Tanis near the tomb of Osorkon II[10] refers to a military expedition. The king is there depicted, like so many of his predecessors, in the act of beating his enemy to death with a club, holding him by the hair. It is unfortunately only a fragment (fig. 5). The explanatory text has disappeared completely and the part showing the enemy has been badly damaged. He is holding a weapon or some object typical of his people. Such a pose was

[10]P. Montet, *Les constructions et le tombeau de Osorkon à Tanis*, Vol. II of *NRT*, pl. IX.

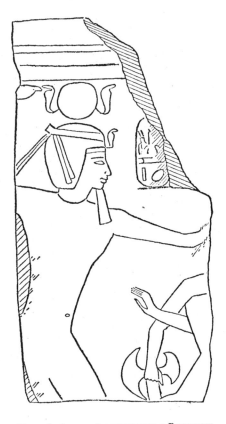

Figure 5. SIAMON SLAUGHTERING A PHILISTINE

characteristic of this type of memorial, but this somewhat enigmatic object bears no similarity to the weapons and tools found in the hands of defeated Syrians, Libyans, or Negroes.[11] I have compared it to the double ax often depicted on Mycenian monuments[12] and have assumed that the defeated man was a Philistine.[13] Our provisional conclusion, then, is that Siamon clashed with the Philistines on the Palestinian coast and that he perhaps intended to march against Israel.

The name of Queen Tahpenes ought to be in either the book of Kings or Ranke's dictionary[14] but such a search proves to be rather disappointing. As H. Gauthier wrote in 1914, we have no information about Siamon's family.[15] The situation has not changed since then. Edouard Dhorme in his recent French translation of the Bible suggests[16] that the name brings to mind the Egyptian city of Tahpanhes that we will discuss in the next chapter. But this resemblance is purely coincidental because in Egyptian the names of cities are never given as such to women. Beginning with Tahpenes, therefore, let us try to go back to an Egyptian original without forgetting that ꜣ can just as easily be the equivalent of *h* as of *ḫ* and that *ḫ* often is equivalent to the Coptic *ch*.[17] It will undoubtedly be readily admitted that it is not far from Tahpenes to Tapehenis and "the part of Isis," to which an Egyptian statue in the Cairo Museum refers. This is

[11]Cf. P. Montet, "L'Arc Nubien et ses emplois dans l'Ecriture," *Kêmi*, VI (1936), 50-52.

[12]René Dussaud, *Les civilisations préhelléniques dans le bassin de la mer Egée* (2nd ed.; Paris: P. Geuthner, 1910), p. 340 (fig. 247).

[13]P. Montet, *DA*, p. 196.

[14]H. Ranke, *Die ägyptischen Personennamen* (2 vols.; Glückstadt: J. J. Augustin, 1935-1952).

[15]Gauthier, *LRE*, III, 298.

[16]E. Dhorme, *L'Ancien Testament*, Vol. 1 of *La Bible* (Bibliothèque NRF de la Pleiade; Paris: Gallimard, 1956), p. 1080, n. 19.

[17]Kurt Sethe, *Das ägyptische Verbum im Altägyptischen, Neuägyptischen und Koptischen* (3 vols.; Leipzig: J. C. Hinrichs, 1899–1902), I, 152-53.

Statue 741, attributed to the XXI dynasty.[18] The metathesis (*ḥp* instead of *pḥ*) is not at all surprising, nor is the use of a ח to render the Egyptian *ḥ* since the latter's pronunciation is not far from a ח. This Tapeheniset was the wife of a great leader of the Maa (an abbreviation of the Maashausha, i.e., Libyans). It will be observed that the Bible does not give the title of "queen" to Tahpenes but only "great lady" (I Kings 11:19). In the second half of the XXI dynasty the great leaders of Ma were already very important figures, until one of them even took possession of Horus' throne.[19] It is perfectly possible that the grandfather or great-grandfather of Sheshonk I did for David's enemy what Sheshonk I later did for Jeroboam, enemy of both Solomon and Rehoboam. He may have advised or even forced a pharaoh who could have been Siamon to welcome Hadad. Hatred for Israel seems to have been endemic in this family.

Somewhat later a sudden change occurred in Egyptian politics that should not surprise us. Solomon became the son-in-law of Pharaoh, king of Egypt (I Kings 3:1). He brought the princess into the city of David. As a dowry she brought him the town of Gezer that Pharaoh had seized. He had destroyed it by fire after having killed the Canaanites who lived there. We have the advantage of knowing that this marriage took place between 980 and 950 and probably at the beginning of the Pharaoh's reign. At that time Pharaoh's throne was occupied by a new Psusennes about whom we have but the sparsest of in-

---

[18]Cf. P. Montet, *DA*, pp. 192-98. In the Septuagint translation Tahpenes becomes Thekemina. Greseloff, no doubt incorrectly, considers the latter to be a transcription of *Ta ḥmt nswt*, "the king's wife" (this title does not require the article). Cf. Bernhard Greseloff, "En marge des récentes recherches sur Tanis," *ASAE*, XLVII (1947), 215.

[19]On the great chiefs of the Ma(šhausha), see Eduard Meyer, *Geschichte des Altertums* (5 vols.; Stuttgart: J. G. Cotta, 1884–1902), II, 30; and Etienne Drioton and Jacques Vandier, *L'Egypte*, p. 523.

formation. Only one daughter is known, Maka-Re, who married Osorkon I who wanted to link his dynasty to the preceding one.[20] It was undoubtedly an elder sister of this princess whom Solomon married. Was it Psusennes II who seized Gezer? No Egyptian document asserts it formally, but we are right in thinking that Gezer, having been captured a few years earlier by Siamon, was given as a dowry to the wife of Solomon by Psusennes II who was incapable of keeping this conquest.

By welcoming Solomon's enemy, Jeroboam (I Kings 11:40), Sheshonk I forecast the great attack against Jerusalem with which we are familiar through I Kings 14:25 and II Chronicles 12:2, 9-11. The fifth year of Rehoboam corresponds to the end of the rule of Sheshonk I who reigned, to the best of our knowledge, for twenty-one years. The invasion army included chariots and horsemen who followed a large number of Libyans, Sukkiites, and Ethiopians. We do not know where the Sukkiites came from. There is nothing unusual about the presence of Ethiopians in Pharaoh's army and even less of Libyans, since Sheshonk I had an ancestor Tehenu who had been the head of the Maa prior to his coronation. The Libyans had already arranged an offensive and defensive alliance with Egypt and were to keep it until the time of Amasis.[21] If King Sheshonk, as is probable, told of this event on a stele, this record has been lost. Nevertheless the great bas-relief which shows Amon offering to the king 155 towns whose names are contained in notched escutcheons can still be seen at Karnak, on the southern façade of the second py-

---

[20]See the inscription on the statue of Prince Sheshonk, son of Osorkon I and Maka-Re in Gaston Maspéro, *Les momies royales de Déir el-Barharî*, Vol. I of *Mémoires de la Mission archéologique française du Caire* (Paris: Ernest Leroux, 1884), I, 734-35.

[21]Libyans were included in Tefnakht's army (Pi-ankhi, 11). On the appeal of the Libyans an Egyptian army under Apries went to attack the king of Cyrene (Herodotus, IV. 159).

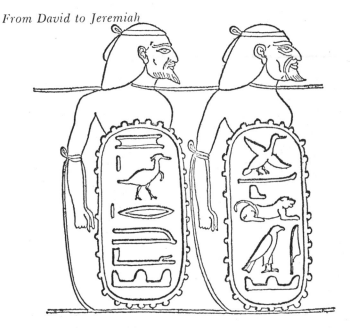

Figure 6. Two of the Towns Conquered by Sheshonk I

lon.[22] Jerusalem, now missing, was probably mentioned on the part that has been lost. Many of the names are spelled in a barbarous way and are hard to identify. Quite interesting is the reference to Abraham's field (fig. 6).[23] When this list is compared to those left by the kings of the New Kingdom, we are forced to recognize that Sheshonk I was far short of duplicating their exploits. Moreover, he had carefully prepared his expedition because a stone bearing his name has been found at Megiddo[24] where the cattle buyer Thut-hotep had lived during the XII dynasty.

[22]Richard Lepsius, *Denkmäler aus Ägypten und Äthiopien* (12 vols.; Berlin: Nicolaische Buchhandlung, 1849–1856), III, 252-53. According to Martin Noth, "Die Shoshenkliste," *Zeitschrift des deutschen Palästina-Vereins,* LXI (1938), 277-304, Sheshonk never entered Jerusalem.

[23]Lepsius, *op. cit.,* III, 252.

[24]Clarence S. Fisher, *The Excavation of Armageddon* ("Oriental Institute Communications," No. 4 [Chicago: University of Chicago Press, 1929]), 12-16; cf. B. van de Walle, *art. cit.,* Vol. IV, cols. 418-82, and J. A. Wilson, *American Journal of Semitic Languages and Literatures,* LVIII (1941), 225-36.

Plate V. Bracelets of Sheshonk I

He had sent his statue to Abibaal, the king of Byblos, who placed it in the temple of the Lady of Byblos after having encircled the escutcheons of the pharaohs with an inscription in Phoenician characters.[25] Thus he could consider Abibaal as an ally.

Two bracelets made of gold and calibrated stones that once belonged to Sheshonk I have come down to us. They

[25]P. Montet, *BE*, No. 31.

were found at Tanis on the mummy of Sheshonk II who had inherited them (pl. V).[26] We cannot help thinking that they might have been made from the gold taken from the Jerusalem temple.

King Asa (911–870 B.C.) successfully drove off the attack of the Ethiopian Zerah (II Chron. 14:9-15; the incident is not mentioned in Kings). Asa could have known Osorkon I, Takelot I, and even Osorkon II at the beginning of his reign. Osorkon I[27] and Osorkon II,[28] like Sheshonk I, sent their statues in homage to the Lady of Byblos. That does not prove that they participated in Zerah's endeavor. However it is unlikely that this Ethiopian could have taken troops through Palestine without having made a treaty with Pharaoh.

The long period which goes from the rule of Osorkon II to Cambyses' conquest of Egypt is marked by great upheaval, reverses, and recoveries that bring to mind the best days of the Amen-hotep and Ramses dynasties. But for the kingdom of Judah this same period was one of anguish, for Egypt primarily brought suffering and disappointment to it.

The king of Assyria had warned Hezekiah that Egypt was a broken reed "on which if a man lean, it will run into his hand and pierce it" (II Kings 18:21). This warning probably occurred at the time of Pharaoh Bocchoris. The prophets echo this harsh judgment:

> Sheer fools are the princes of Zoan (Tanis; cf.
> pl. VI),
> The wisest of Pharaoh's counselors are a senseless
> council (Isa. 19:11).
> Deluded are the princes of Memphis (Noph) (Isa.
> 19:13).

[26]P. Montet, *Les constructions et le tombeau de Psousennès,* colored pls., Nos. 226-27.

[27]P. Montet, *BE,* Nos. 26-30.

[28]Maurice Dunand, *Fouilles de Byblos* (Paris: P. Geuthner, 1937), No. 1741.

Plate VI. MASK AND WRAPPINGS OF A PRINCE OF TANIS CALLED SHESHONK II, GRANDSON OF SHESHONK I

44

Egypt seemed to them to be in desperate straits. Here is how Jeremiah pictures Yahweh speaking:

> Behold, Amon of Thebes will I punish,
> And Pharaoh, and those who trust in him" (Jer. 46:25).

Isaiah had said:

> Woe to you rebellious children . . .
> Who carry out a purpose that comes not from me,
> And who form an alliance that is not according to
>   my mind . . .
> Who set out on the way to Egypt,
> Without asking my advice,
> To take refuge in the protection of Pharaoh,
> And to take shelter in the shadow of Egypt!"
> (Isa. 30:1-2).

And later (Isa. 30:7):

> To Egypt, whose help is empty and vain,
> Wherefore I have called her "Rahab Sit-still."
>   (lit., a noise that ends in nothing)

Again Jeremiah asks:

> Now what business have you on the road to Egypt,
> To drink the water of the Nile? (Jer. 2:18).

In spite of these warnings those who took refuge in Egypt at the time of the terrible Nebuchadnezzar were numerous:

> Then all the people, both small and great, and the commanders of the forces arose and came to Egypt; for they were afraid of the Chaldeans (II Kings 25:26).

The prophets were obliged to recognize this fact (Jer. 44:16-17), and Jeremiah who had so eloquently predicted shame and misfortune for those who went to Egypt ended up being taken there himself (Jer. 43:4-7).

On the Egyptian side evidence is rare and reserved. When Hoshea was defeated by Shalmaneser V, he had, according to II Kings 17:4, the unfortunate idea of sending messages to Sewe, king of Egypt. This name is not familiar to the book of Kings. The Annals of Sargon, however, reveal that Sewe (Sib'e) was only a general. At that time there was no real pharaoh.[29]

No record in the Egyptian tongue mentions Sennacherib's undertaking in 701 B.C., that was halted by an angel (II Kings 19:35; II Chron. 32:21). Herodotus tells the story in his own way. The king of Egypt at the time was a priest of Ptah by the name of Sethos. Abandoned by his forces he went to Pelusium accompanied by shopkeepers and common people. The god Ptah spread a hoard of rats over the countryside so that the enemy took flight and perished in large numbers.[30] Modern historians prosaically explain that Sennacherib's flight was caused by an epidemic.

The reign of Necho, the second king of that name (609–594 B.C.)[31] was certainly a glorious one, although defeat at Carchemish cost him all his Asian conquests in a single blow. It so happens that his major undertakings (the Asian campaigns, the excavation of the Red Sea canal, the African tour) are known above all through the Bible, Herodotus, and Diodorus. However an architectural fragment found at Sidon and imprints found at Carchemish are indisputable traces of the presence of Egyptians in these two cities at the time of Necho.

Deaf to the warnings of the prophet Jeremiah, Jehoiakim remained faithful to the Egyptian alliance (II Kings 23:34-35). It seems that Necho made a kind of recovery after the defeat of Carchemish. He was in fact victorious at Magdolus, and captured Cadytis.[32] Herodotus' last

[29]Cf. *ANET*, p. 285 and nn. 3, 4. The reign of Shalmaneser V (726-712 B.C.) corresponds to a very obscure period in Egyptian history. Tefnakht, Prince of Saïs, endeavored to increase the size of his domain and Pi-ankhi, having conquered all Egypt with the exception of the northern part of the Delta, withdrew to the South.
[30]Herodotus, II. 141.
[31]J. Yoyotte, "Nechao," *DBS*, Vol. VI, cols. 368-92.
[32]Herodotus, II. 159.

editor and other scholars consider Magdolus a mistake for what should have been Megiddo. Nothing needs to be changed. Magdolus certainly corresponds to one of the *Mktr,* citadels of the Syrian type that existed in Egypt itself and on the military road from Sile to Hebron,[33] very likely at this latter site. Cadytis is Gaza which Pharaoh struck just as the prophet Jeremiah had predicted (Jer. 47:1) when he spoke of the Philistines.

One of Necho's successors is also mentioned in Jeremiah 44:30. He is Hophra whom Yahweh will deliver "into the hand of his enemies, into the hand of those who seek his life." It is easy to recognize Hophra as Pharaoh *Wah-ib-Re,* whom the Greeks called Apries.[34] This king led an expedition against Tyre and Sidon, whose destruction had been predicted by Jeremiah (Jer. 47:4).[35] But, as Herodotus continues, misfortune had to strike. His downfall came, not from the Sidonians or the Jews, but from Libya.

But that is another story.

[33]Cf. *JEA,* VI (1920), pl. XI (opposite p. 100).
[34]Herodotus, II. 161.
[35]*Ibid.,* IV. 159.

4

Egypt's Geography

AS DEPICTED IN THE BIBLE

In the preceding chapters we have mentioned a number of regions and towns in Egypt. Many other geographical expressions are encountered in the Bible. We propose to study them in this chapter by going from the north to the south of Egypt (fig. 7).

1. MAZOR is the Hebrew name for Egypt, most frequently encountered in the dual form, "Mizraim" (cf. II Kings 19:24). Egyptians called their country *Kmt,* "Kêmi," the Black; or *Ta Kmy,* the Black Land.[1] They also had a number of other ways of describing it: *Ta mry,* the Beloved Land; *Tawy,* the Two Lands; and *idbwy,* the Two Rivers, names that not only the Hebrews but all Semitic languages deliberately ignore. "Masr" still today refers to both Egypt and its capital.

Another land called *Musri* in Hebrew is mentioned in I Kings 10:28 as the land that provided horses and chariots for Solomon. It has been placed in Cilicia.[2] Other lands both in the Mesopotamian East and in Arabia have also been designated "Musur." They are all situated on the

---

[1] P. Montet, *To-mehou . . . , GEA,* I, pp. 4-5.
[2] Edouard Dhorme, *La Bible* (Bibliothèque NRF de la Pleiade; Paris: Gallimard, 1956), I, 1077, n. 28; cf. also A. S. Kapelrud, "Mizraim," in *IDB,* III, 409.

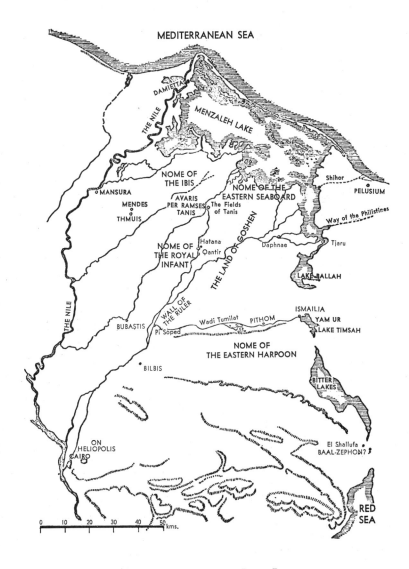

Figure 7. Map of the Eastern Delta Region

49

periphery of the Semitic world.[3] It may therefore be admitted that the Semites called lands that they could consider as some distance away by the name "Muṣur."

2. YEOR, the Hebrew word for "Nile" in Pharaoh's dream (Gen. 41:1), corresponds perfectly with the Egyptian *ỉtrw*, "a river" in general, and specifically "the Nile." The *t* has not been retained in either Hebrew or Coptic, and even in Egypt forms without the *t* occur from the beginning of the XVIII dynasty on. It is good to keep this fact in mind, as well as other clues to which we have drawn attention to date the time when the Bible was written.

The Egyptians were quite willing to call their river *Ḥ'apy*, above all when they apotheosized it or during a flood, when it stretched from one cliff to the other and turned every town and village into an island or islet.

3. THE SHI-HOR (River of Egypt) which forms part of the eastern border of Egypt (Josh. 13:3, 5; I Chron. 13:5) is a transliteration of the Egyptian *Shi-Hor,* literally "the reservoir of Horus." It is the canal in which the Eastern Seaboard Nome's sacred bark was docked.[4] It irrigated the capital of this nome, Tjaru (Sile), in the Kantarah district, and other cities such as Daphnae and Pelusium constructed along the eastern border. From this canal the royal residence at Per-Ramses could be reached and provided with reeds and salt.[5] Thus it corresponds perfectly with the lower course of the Nile's Pelusiac branch.

It may seem surprising that a branch of the Nile is designated by a term that is more suited to a vast expanse of water, but the names of the Mediterranean and Red Seas (Yam and Wadj Wer, the "Great Green") likewise refer to certain branches of the Nile in Upper Egypt.

[3]P. Garelli, "Musur," in *DBS,* Vol. V, cols. 1468–74.
[4]P. Montet, *GEA,* I, p. 200.
[5]P. Montet, *DA,* 117-18.

Moreover it is possible that Shi-Hor really was the name of a lake and, by extension, of the branch of the Nile that went through it. A good possibility would be Lake Ballah, not far from the towns of Mesen and Tjaru and the Ways of Horus outpost.

4. SIN, Σαϊν in the Septuagint and Pelusium in the Vulgate, is mentioned in Ezekiel 30:15. "I will pour out my fury on Pelusium, the stronghold of Egypt," the prophet says. Pelusium is also considered by Greek authors as Egypt's port.[6] Corresponding to Sin is the Egyptian *Snw*, one of the five winegrowing districts of the map, located by one papyrus at the land's farthest border.[7]

5. TAHPANHES is the city to which Jeremiah was taken and where many Jews had already found refuge (Jer. 43:7-8). The Septuagint transcribes this name as Ταφνάι, a name which corresponds to the Pelusian "Daphne" of Herodotus[8] and to the modern Tell Defneh located on the Pelusiac branch of the Nile, slightly to the west of the Suez Canal. The Egyptian name of this town appears to have been *Tjeben*.[9] The site has been explored by Flinders Petrie.[10] The objects discovered do not go back beyond the Saïtic era. The numerous Greek potsherds confirm the facts as given by Herodotus. An edifice made of rough brick is curiously called the Castle of the Jew's Daughter, no doubt in memory of the Jewish emigration.[11] Jeremiah 43:9 speaks of a brick pavement in the gateway of Pharaoh's palace at Tahpanhes. To be sure, the site has not been completely excavated and until now nothing

---

[6]Cf. Herodotus, II. 141 and Josephus, *Against Apion* I. 274, 291.
[7]P. Montet, *GEA*, I, 191.
[8]Herodotus, II. 30, 154.
[9]P. Montet, *GEA*, I, 191.
[10]W. M. F. Petrie, *Tanis* (2 vols.; London: Trübner and Co., 1888–1889), II, 47-96 and pl. XLIII.
[11]*Ibid.*, II, 52-53 and pl. XLIV. Our mission discovered a similar type of monument at Tanis; cf. M. Fougerousse in Pierre Montet, *Les nouvelles fouilles de Tanis: 1929–1932* (Paris and Strasbourg: Les Belles-Lettres, 1933), chap. iii. It was just as enigmatic as the one at Defneh.

has been pointed out that could be the remains of a royal palace. It is unlikely that any pharaoh would have had a residence built at Defneh, but perhaps Jeremiah has called the home of the local governor the royal palace. There undoubtedly does exist in the town a reminder of the Jewish emigration — a stele found at Defneh showing a figure perched on a pedestal to worship a god crowned with a tiara and standing on a lion. The scene is lighted by a full moon and two crescents.[12]

If Ταφνάι had been transcribed according to the Egyptian *Tjben,* the name Tahpanhes with its two п 's calls for an explanation. If we transcribe it letter by letter we get a very plausible form, *Ta ḥwt pa nḥs,* "temple of the Nubian." But no place in Egypt with which I am familiar has such a name. Nevertheless this expression would be very suitable for a shrine to the god Min who, often painted black, could merit the name "Negro."[13] This god is well-known in the eastern region of the Delta, at San el-Hagar and Nebeshe. He is even specifically mentioned on a stele found at Defneh.[14]

6. ZOAN is the Egyptian town of Djaʿaney, the Greek Τανις, whose ruins are at the San el-Hagar tell. According to Numbers 13:22 Zoan was built seven years later than Hebron. Unfortunately we do not know when this latter town was built. The name Tanis first appears in the story of Wen-amon, the navigator sent by Smendes at the beginning of the XXI dynasty to negotiate the purchase of some wood from Zekerbaal, king of Byblos. At San el-Hagar there no doubt are many monuments that are much,

[12]W. Max Müller, "The Local Semitic God of the Biblical Tahpanhes," *Egyptological Researches* (3 vols.; Washington: Carnegie Institute, 1906–1920) , I, 30-31 and pl. XL.

[13]Henri Gauthier, *Les fêtes du dieu Min* (Cairo: Imprimerie de l'Institut français d'archéologie orientale, 1931) , 201-2. But cf. T. O. Lambdin, "Tahpanhes," in *IDB,* IV, 510.

[14]Petrie, *op. cit.,* II, pl. XLII.

much older but they belong to two towns that preceded Tanis on the same spot — namely Avaris, where the pharaoh who welcomed Joseph resided; and Per-Ramses, to be mentioned later.

Smendes' successors continued to live at Tanis. The one who made the greatest contribution to the improvement of the city was Psusennes whose unspoiled tomb our mission discovered. To protect his residence and his tomb he had a strong wall built whose bricks all bear his seal.[15] Tanis remained the royal residence until the XXVI dynasty.[16] The prophets speak scornfully of its princes (Isa. 19:11, 13) and include it in the general curse which they pronounce against Egypt (Ezek. 30:14).

The expression Sedeh Ṣo'an, "the fields of Zoan" (Ps. 78:12, 43), LXX πεδιον Τανεως, is a literal translation from the Egyptian *Sekhet-Dja'any,* "Tanis Prairie," the later form of *Sekhet-Dja'a,* "Djaa Prairie." This last-mentioned form denotes a geographical setting appropriate to Tanis where there are cultivated areas protected by dikes against flooding. Djaa Prairie was a district in the Eastern Seaboard that already included Avaris and Per-Ramses. When Smendes founded his new town, he called it Djaaney, the town of the djaa, and later Djaa Prairie became Tanis Prairie.[17] Prior to the Exodus this prairie was the theater for a number of exciting events.

7. RAMSES is mentioned twice in the Bible. In Exodus 1:11 the new king who did not know Joseph had the towns of Pithom and Ramses built to serve as his store-cities. In Genesis 47:11 the land granted to the sons of Israel,

---

[15]P. Montet, *Les constructions et le tombeau de Psousennès,* Vol. II of *NRT,* p. 12.

[16]The last or one of the last to bear the name Sheshonk built a spacious temple and a jubilee building at Tanis. Our mission recovered many stone blocks from the latter. A Tirhakah stele attests to the eminent role of Tanis during this pharaoh's reign; cf. J. Leclant et J. Yoyotte, "Nouveaux documents relatifs á l'an VI de Taharqa," *Kêmi,* X (1950), 37.

[17]Cf. P. Montet, *GEA,* I, 201.

Figure 8. THE GOD SETH OF RAMSES (STELE OF THE YEAR 400)

always called Goshen elsewhere, is described as the land of Ramses. This land was none other than the residence that Ramses II had founded east of the Delta and frequently mentioned in Egyptian texts.[18] Its complete name is *Per-Ramses-mry 'Imn 'aa neḥtw,* "the dwelling of Ramses beloved of Amon the great Victor," but it can be shortened not only by the elimination of the epithets, but also by the omission of the component *pr,* "dwelling." Many geographical expressions used by the Egyptians and composed of *pr,* "dwelling," and *ḥwt,* "castle," were occasionally

---

[18]Cf. A. H. Gardiner, "The Delta Residence of the Ramessides," *JEA,* V (1918), 127-38, 179-200, 242-71; and *ibid.,* "The Geography of the Exodus," X (1924), 93-94.

dropped, just as the Hebrew Beth-baal-meon (Josh. 13:17) is abbreviated Baal-meon (Num. 32:38). It is customary to drop the *pr* when Per-Ramses is used in a title such as "royal son of Ramses"[19] or the name of a god. In granite columns, on the pedestals of statues and bas-reliefs it is said that the king is beloved of the gods of Ramses — Seth (fig. 8), Amon, Pre, Ptah, Tem (Atum), Anta, and Wadjit — in precisely the place where on other monuments it is said that the king is beloved of Ptah of Memphis or Min of Coptos.[20] Each example of these gods — and they are numerous — proves that at San el-Hagar we are on the site of Per-Ramses or, through abbreviation, Ramses.

Even more convincing is a description of the San el-Hagar tell that contains more monuments of Ramses II and his immediate succesors than any other site in Lower Egypt (pl. VII).[21] At Per-Ramses the great king built jubilee castles, just as his imitator, Ramses III, would do later. We discovered more than just a trace of these castles at San el-Hagar. One discoverey was a magnificent flagstone six meters long. In the vault of Psusennes we found a piece of personal property, a small portable bronze stove, that comes direct from it.[22]

Na-Ramses on the banks of the Pety Canal belonged to Per-Ramses. It corresponds perfectly with what the Bible

[19]The "royal sons of Ramses" were the governors of (Per-) Ramses, just as the royal sons of Kush, El-Kab, and This governed territories or towns with those names. They were chosen from the reigning family (XXII dynasty) and in no way descended from Ramses as has sometimes been said, e.g., by Henri Gauthier, "Variétiés historiques," *ASAE*, XVIII (1918), 245; cf. also B. Couroyer, "La résidence Ramesside du Delta et la Ramsès biblique," *RB*, LIII (1946), 75-98.

[20]P. Montet, "Les dieux de Ramsès aimé d'Amon," in *Studies Presented to F. Lloyd Griffiths*, ed. S. R. K. Glanville (London: Egyptian Exploration Society; H. Milford, Oxford University Press, 1932), p. 406. The opposite opinion will be found in Alan H. Gardiner, "Tanis and Pi-Ramesse," *JEA*, XIX (1933), 124; and B. Couroyer, "Peuples voisins: Egypte," *RB*, XLV (1936), 150-55.

[21]P. Montet, *Les énigmes de Tanis* (Paris: Payot, 1952), 66, 86, 101.

[22]P. Montet, "Écrit à Tanis en 1956," *Revue archéologique*, I (1958), 1-20.

Plate VII. BLOCK FROM RAMSES II'S PALACE DECORATED WITH THE HEADS OF
PRISONERS (THE BLOCK WAS REUSED IN TANIS'S MONUMENTAL DOOR)

56

calls Pharaoh's store-city,[23] and a cemetery, the *ḥr* of Ramses.[24] The kings of the XIX dynasty whose remains lay in the Valley of the Kings of Thebes also kept "tombs" in their northern residence. Mer-ne-Ptah's sarcophagus, usurped by Psusennes, comes from one of these so-called tombs.

Constructed for an endless period of time, this town was completely sacked during the War of the Unclean. When Smendes rebuilt it, he changed its name to Tanis. Memory of its earlier name did not disappear overnight however. The kings of the XXII dynasty instituted the "royal sons of Ramses" and among the gods of Ramses Amon still had a priesthood in the Lower Epoch.[25]

8. PITHOM, another store-city built by Pharaoh (Exod. 1:11) is quite properly transcribed from the Egyptian *Pr-'Itm,* "house of the god Tem (Atum) ," the capital of the Eastern Harpoon and known under the name of *Tkw,* Tjeku.[26] Its remains are at Tell el-Maskhuteh, a site which has not been the object of systematic excavations. The *sebhakhin* have been guilty of much destruction. Its many stone monuments are the pride of the stele gardens at *Ismailiyeh.* A sphinx and a monument from the Middle Kingdom have been usurped, the first by the Hyksos, the second by Seti I. A naos and some triads date from the time of Ramses II. Some red brick buildings have been identified as the stores built by the sons of Israel,[27] but this view must be abandoned once and for all.

9. GOSHEN (Gen. 45:10; 46:28; 47:1; Exod. 8:22; 9:26). The land of Goshen in which Joseph and Pharaoh

[23]A. H. Gardiner, "The Delta Residence of the Ramessides," *JEA,* V (1918) , 188, No. 18.

[24]*Ibid.,* V (1918) , 197, No. 35.

[25]P. Montet, "Trois Gouverneurs de Tanis d'après les inscriptions des statues 687, 689 et 700 du Caire," *Kêmi,* VII (1938), 143, 157.

[26]P. Montet, *GEA,* I, 213.

[27]Petrie, *op. cit.,* I, pl. XVI.

placed Jacob's sons was a large area suitable for the raising of sheep, an area in which the tribe thrived year after year. It was very close to Avaris, the capital of the king who welcomed the refugees; it was also near the oppressor's residence, Per-Ramses, located on the same spot. This explains why the Chronicler, undoubtedly writing long after the Exodus, wrote on one occasion "land of Ramses" instead of "land of Goshen."

The land of Goshen probably extended to Pithom in the south and to *Gsm* (Gesem), the town that gave the land its name, in the west. The name appears for the first time in a hymn in which Sen-Wesret III is described as *"Gesem's* copper bulwark."[28] This means "a bulwark that is as solid as the copper at Gesem" and not "a bulwark made of Gesem copper." This bulwark is none other than the famous Wall-of-the-Ruler built by Amen-em-het I at the very edge of the cultivated land of Egypt.[29] The location of *Gsm* is indicated more exactly by the naos of Nectanebo I, found at Saft el Henneh. To honor his father Soped, lord of the East, this king came to *Gsmt* to contemplate this august god in his temple and to put the statue of this god of *Gsm* in this naos.[30] In the temple at Edfu the geographical figure symbolizing the Soped Nome says that he cares for the Soped Nome and the town of *Gesem*.[31] Just as Pithom was also called Tjeku, the capital of the Soped Nome (whose ruins are at Saft el Henneh) had

[28]F. Llewellyn Griffith, *The Petrie Papyri: Hieratic Papyri from Kahun and Gurob* (2 vols.; London: B. Quaritch, 1898), I, pl. II, 2, 14.
[29]The Wall-of-the-Ruler is mentioned in the Ermitage (Leningrad) Papyrus 1116B: G. Lefebvre, *RCE*, p. 104; and *Si-nuhe* R42: *ibid.*, p. 7. G. Posener, *Littérature et politique dans l'Egypte de la XIIe dynastie* (Paris: H. Champion, 1956), pp. 54-57, places this wall in Wadi Tumilat, but more to the east, toward Pithom; Lefebvre places it, as we do, at the entrance to the Wadi (*op. cit.*, p. 7, No. 20).
[30]Edouard Naville, *The Shrine of Saft el Henneh and the Land of Goshen* (London: Trübner and Co., 1887), pl. VI.
[31]E. G. Chassinat, *Deux bas-reliefs historiques du temple d'Edfu* (Cairo: 1939), VI, 42. For a similar text at Dendara, cf. Johannes Dümichen, *Geographische Inschschriften altägyptischer Dënkmaler an Ort und Stelle* (4 vols.; Leipzig: J. C. Hinrichs, 1865–1885), III, 25.

two names: Per-Sopcd ("Soped's dwelling") and Gesem.

A very serious problem arises concerning the initial symbol which can be read in two different ways, *g* or *shes*. The letter *g* (V, 33 of Gardiner's list) represents a full sack that is wider at one end than the other, and the sign *shes* (V, 6 in the same list), one end of a rope that is hollow and equal at both ends. On the inscriptions on the monuments these two signs are quite dissimilar but they are confused in hieratic writing and in many hieroglyphic inscriptions.[32] Gardiner[33] and Newberry[34] preferred the reading *shesm*, or *shesmet* to the reading *Gsm* lauded by Brugsch.[35] It can not be denied that the god Soped is also the lord of a district in Sinai called *Ta shesmt*, "the land of the mineral *shesmt*," probably malachite. Thus it may be supposed that the name *shesm* or *shesmt* was given to Per-Soped because the caravans which went to work the malachite at Sinai left from this point. This is an interesting hypothesis we must resort to if we choose the reading *shesmt*, but it is unverifiable. But if the reading *Gsm* is chosen we are in familiar territory and it cannot be doubted, as Brugsch thought at first, that this *Gsm* is the original form of Goshen in the Septuagint.

The land of Goshen can be located even more specifically by determining the site of a third point, Per-Soped. The Wall-of-the-Ruler, solid as copper and built somewhat to the east of this city, separated the land of Goshen from Egypt proper.[36]

---

[32]A. H. Gardiner, *Egyptian Grammar* (2nd ed.; London: G. Cumberlege, 1950), p. 523, V, 6.

[33]A. H. Gardiner, "The Supposed Egyptian Equivalent of the Name of Goshen," *JEA*, V (1918), 218.

[34]Percy E. Newberry, "Ssnt," in Glanville, *op. cit.*, p. 321.

[35]H. K. Brugsch, "Die Götter des Nomos Arabias," *ZÄS*, XIX (1881), 15-18.

[36]An allusion to this Wall occurs in the accounts of naos 2248 of Ismailiyeh which comes from Per-Soped. Cf. Georges Goyon, "Les Travaux de Chou et les tribulations de Geb d'après le naos 2248 d'Ismaïlia," *Kêmi*, VI (1936), 28.

10. THE STOPS ALONG THE ROUTE OF THE EXODUS. The best route for going to Syria was that which went from Tjaru, the main city in the Eastern Seaboard, and which was dotted by fortresses built in the neighborhood of the principal watering spots as far as Pa-Canaan.[37] To have taken it would in fact have been a mistake because it was watched even in times of peace. It is this route over which the armies of Thut-mose III, Seti I, and Ramses II had marched. Moreover, Elohim had suggested to the sons of Israel not to take the route of the Philistines even though it was close, but to take the desert route by way of the Sea of Reeds (Exod. 13:17-18).

It is this latter route that fugitives took instinctively. Two examples are known. First of all Si-nuhe, having left his post in the Libyan army, managed to reach the region of On and passed to the east of the sandstone quarry. Veering toward the north he approached the Wall-of-the-Ruler, taking care not to show himself to the sentinels. Marching at night he reached an unknown spot called Peten without encountering any opposition and arrived completely exhausted at an island in the Land of the Great Black called Lake Timsah where he received aid.[38]

The other example is the report of a police officer from Tjeku (Pithom) under Seti II charged with following two fugitive slaves: "From the main hall of the royal palace (at Per-Ramses) — may he live, be prosperous, be healthy — I was sent at the third month of summer at nine o'clock in the evening to pursue two slaves. So I reached the walls of Tjeku on the tenth day of the third month. I was told that they had been sighted passing toward the south on

[37]A. H. Gardiner, "The Ancient Military Road Between Egypt and Palestine," *JEA*, VI (1920), 99.

[38]"The Story of Si-nuhe," trans. John A. Wilson, in James B. Pritchard, *ANET*, pp. 18-22.

the tenth. Then I came to the fortress *(khetem)* and I was told that a courier had come from the desert saying that they had passed the Wall-of-the-Ruler, to the north of the Migdol of Seti-Mer-ne-Ptah—may he live, be prosperous, be healthy—beloved like Seth. When this letter reaches you, let me know all that has happened to them."[39]

The word *sgr*, which corresponds to the Hebrew *segor*, denotes a kind of castle which should not be confused with *khetem*, a fortress of a purely Egyptian type, nor with the *migdol*, a building of a Syrian type like the fortified gate of Medinet Habu. These three buildings which existed in the region of Tjeku cannot be located exactly on the map. Any comparison with the stopping places of the sons of Israel will therefore be more theoretical than factual.

The first stopping place of the sons of Israel (Exod. 12:37; Num. 33:3-5), Ramses-succoth, inevitably leads to a consideration of the distance that the Egyptian police officer travelled in one night from the royal palace to the walls of Tjeku. Some scholars have even identified Succoth with *Theku*.[40] But this identification is not satisfying from a phonetic point of view and it is hard to see the sons of Israel going to Pithom, capital of a nome, where the governor who had an armed force at his command resided. Even if this force was not large enough to stop them, it would have been large enough to make them uneasy. The common name Succoth, which means huts or booths in Hebrew, could be compared to certain Egyptian geographical expressions formed with *ta wḥyt,* "the tribe," or *ta ỉh,* "the encampment," used to the west of Ahnas in a region frequented by nomads. Succoth could be an en-

[39]"The Pursuit of Runaway Slaves," *ibid.,* pp. 259. Wilson's translation differs slightly.
[40]Papyrus Anastasi, V, 19, 6-20; cf. Alan H. Gardiner, "The Geography of the Exodus: An Answer to Professor Naville and Others," *JEA,* X (1924), 89, and Pierre Montet *DA,* p. 150.

campment surrounded by a barricade and corresponding to the *sgr* of *Tjekw.*

Etham, that the sons of Israel reached next, is located on the edge of the desert (Exod. 13:20), and could correspond to *khetem.* Although the comparison of the two words is not completely satisfying, I still prefer this identification to the one suggested by Edouard Dhorme — with the god Atum — because the name *Per-itm* is correctly translated "Pithom" in Exodus 1:11.[41]

Having reached this *khetem,* the sons of Israel had only to continue their march into the desert, it would seem. However, according to Numbers 33:7, they came back to Pi-haḥirot opposite Baal-zephon and camped in front of Migdol, but it is from Pi-haḥirot that they left to cross the Sea of Reeds. According to Exodus 14:2, they camped at only one spot, Pi-haḥirot, before reaching the sea. The two other names only serve to locate Pi-haḥirot more specifically between Migdol and the sea opposite Baal-zephon.

It is tempting to identify Migdol on the one hand with the *migdol* (fortress) of Seti-Mer-ne-Ptah, and on the other hand with the town mentioned in Jeremiah 44:1; 46:14; Exodus 14:2, and Numbers 33:7, where the Jews who were fleeing their country gathered, not far from the border. But for lack of any archaeological evidence the position of this *migdol* is not certain. It cannot even be affirmed that there was only a single *migdol* in the area.

Baal-zephon is a god known to the Egyptians; he is involved in a text on the wonders of Memphis where he had a temple,[42] and in a stele found at Ugarit.[43] In principle the name of a god is not a geographical name, but nothing prevents us from admitting that the complete name was Beth-baal-zephon and that the first part has been omitted as in the case of Ramses.

---

[41]Dhorme, *op. cit.,* I, 213.
[42]Papyrus Sallier, IV, Nos. 1, 6, in Alan H. Gardiner, *Late-Egyptian Miscellanies,* Vol. VII in *BA,* p. 89.
[43]Cf. *Syria,* XVIII (1937), pl. VI; and *Kêmi,* VII (1938), 182.

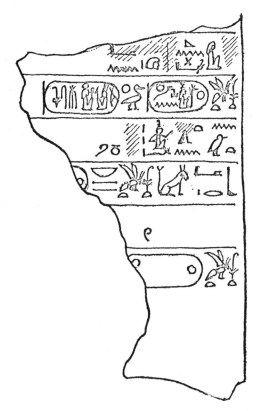

Figure 9. Baal, Mentioned on a Stele of Ramses II at Gebel Shaduf

To locate this stop, Baal-zephon, we have only a very slight indication in one of the two stelae found by Clédat at *Gebel Shaduf*.[44] On one surface, Ramses II is paying homage to Soped, lord of the East. On the opposite surface, which is very worn, he is perhaps honoring Baal-zephon — the name Baal occurs at the beginning of a line in the inscription which constitutes the commentary on the scene (cf. fig. 9).

[44]Cf. *Kêmi* VII (1938), pl. XX. A lake containing fish in the region bears a name composed with Baal; cf. Alan H. Gardiner, "The Delta Residence of the Ramessides," *JEA*, V (1918), 185.

It is not impossible that Pi-hahirot, sometimes abbreviated Hirot, is a somewhat fantastic transcription of *Pr Hwt-Hr,* "the dwelling of Hathor." A town by this name is mentioned in the eulogy on Per-Ramses composed by the scribe Pabasa[45] and in the stele of Nitocris.[46] It furnished papyrus, it seems. We have at our command only very inadequate evidence on which to assign its locality, the discovery near Gebel Shaduf of a small building containing two examples of the name of the Lady of the Turquoises.[47] But one can include in the possibilities *Hwt Hwt-Hr,* "the castle of Hathor," located in the agricultural territory of the nome;[48] and *Pr krht* quoted in the Pithom stele[49] and even *Pkhartî* on the route from Per-Soped to Memphis.[50]

The Sea of Reeds, *Yam Suph,* mentioned for the first time in Exodus 10:19, reminds Egyptologists of *Pa twfy,* which refers to (a) an area situated between Tanis and Tjaru and (b) a canal filled with papyri (just as the Shi-Hor yielded reeds).[51]

The results of our inquiry may disappoint the reader. The isthmus region has not yielded many ancient monuments and those which do exist are in terrible condition. Cities which were once inhabited have completely disappeared. Perhaps archaeological discoveries will one day augment our knowledge. A recently published papy-

[45]Papyrus Anastasi, III, 3, 3, in Alan H. Gardiner, *op. cit.,* p. 23.

[46]Line 25 in Georges Legrain, "Deux stèles trouvées à Karnak en février, 1897," *ZAS,* XXXV (1897), 18.

[47]Jean Clédat, "Notes sur l'Isthme de Suez," *Bulletin de l'Institut français d'archéologie orientale du Caire,* XVI (1919), 208-12, 219.

[48]E. G. Chassinat, *Le temple de Dendera* (5 vols.; Cairo: Imprimerie de l'Institut français d'archéologie orientale, 1934–1947), I, 125.

[49]P. Montet, *GEA,* I, 216.

[50]Goyon, *art. cit.,* p. 14.

[51]P. Montet, *GEA,* I, 200. Egyptians often paralleled a northern name with a southern name. Shi-Hor, which flows into the Mediterranean, could therefore be paralleled with the Reed Canal which springs from the Sea of Reeds.

rus, Papyrus Jumilhac,[52] will furnish us with unhoped for information on what has until now been one of the least known regions of ancient Egypt. A text of this kind which will tell us something about the region that the sons of Israel crossed is assuredly welcome.

11. PER-BESETH (Ezek. 30:17) corresponds to *Pr-Bastt,* βουβαστις in Greek, "Bastet's dwelling." The ancient form was *Bast.* From this form arose *Bastt,* "the goddess Bastet," i.e. "she who comes from Bast"; and *Pr-Bastt.*

12. ON (Gen. 41:45, 50; 46:20) is the land of Joseph's father-in-law. Its Egyptian name *iwnw* became *Ôn* in Coptic. Ezekiel united it with Per-Beseth and Noph in a curse (Ezek. 30:13, 17; cf. also Jer. 46:14). We can recognize *Mnnfr* (Mennofer, Μεμφις) as Noph if we cut off the initial part. The final *r* was no longer pronounced. The northern capital included a large number of foreigners, and Jews would certainly be included when hard times struck their homeland.

13. PATHROS (Ezek. 29:14, 15), *Ptores* in Coptic, is quite correctly transcribed *pa ta rsy,* "the land of the South," i.e., Upper Egypt (also called *ta shem ȧw*).

14. HANES (Isa. 30:4) is an important city in Middle Egypt, *Ḥwt Nn-Sw,* "the Castle of the Reed Children," which became *Ḥininši* in Assyrian, *Hnes* in Coptic, and *Ahnas* in Arabic, and which was reached by the Jewish emigrants.

15. NO (Jer. 46:25; Ezek. 30:14-16) is none other than Thebes, also called *Niwt 'Imn,* "the City of Amon," *Niwt rst,* "the City of the South" and simply *Niwt,* "the City."[53]

16. SEWENEH (Ezek. 29:10; 30:6) is Syene, in the first nome of Upper Egypt across from the island of Elephan-

---

[52]J. Vandier, *Le Papyrus Jumilhac* (Paris: Centre nationale de recherche scientifique, 1961).

[53]Kurt Sethe, *Amun und die acht Urgötter von Hermopolis* (Berlin: Verlag der Akademie der Wissenschaften, 1929), pp. 1-2.

tine, where a Jewish colony settled around 630 B.C.[54]

The list of Egyptian geographical names quoted in the Bible is strictly limited to the events which interest Israel: the settling of the sons of Jacob, the persecution which followed, the Exodus, and finally the emigration that began with the Assyrian invasion.

[54]A. Vincent, *La religion des Judéo-Araméens d'Eléphantine* (Paris: P. Geuthner, 1937).

PART TWO
CULTURAL MATTERS

5

Egyptian Customs in the Bible

PHARAOH AND GOVERNMENT

The pharaoh pictured in Genesis is a paternalistic ruler. He is easily approached and nothing is solemn about the audiences he grants. He is preoccupied with his dreams. He accepts, and even solicits, advice. Yet, at the same time, he is quite capable of flaring up against his servants. We are not told why he deals mercilessly with one and pardons another; perhaps he does so very casually and for reasons arising from personal friendship, or perhaps on the other hand because religious rules had been infringed upon. In brief, he is not very different from the pharaoh that we see throughout the Westcar papyrus, Cheops, who listen to stories and then, following a prediction, is preoccupied with the future.[1]

The story of Si-nuhe presents us with a much more imposing pharaoh. Not everyone who wanted to approach him did so. Those who received an official invitation made themselves known at the palace, and when the proper time came, they entered trembling before the king, and were introduced by the princes; they had to flatten them-

[1]G. Lefebvre, *RCE*, p. 74.

Figure 10. A Royal Audience in the XVIII Dynasty

selves on the ground, and not arise to speak until they were given an express order to do so.[2]

During the XVIII dynasty, court ceremonial continues to be very imposing. A painting from this period repre- sents Prince Kha-monwas being received by Amen-hotep III (fig. 10).[3] The Prince, bowing slightly, is standing at ground level with a petition in his hand. Pharaoh, adorned like an idol, his insignia in his hands, is seated on his throne, raised above ground level by a platform over which is a gold-covered wooden superstructure. The great Ramses seems to have been more accessible, at least when he stayed at his favorite residence, because the scribe, Pa- basa, in his eulogy on Per-Ramses, notes that men stood at their doors on the day when User-maat-Re arrived and that everyone was an equal in making his request to him: the poor man was treated the same as the rich man.[4] That is exactly what happened when Moses dared to approach Pharaoh after Yahweh said to him, "Go to Pharaoh in the morning, just as he is leaving the water; take your stand on the banks of the Nile . . . and . . . say to him . . ." (Exod. 7:15-16) .

The king's entourage that welcomed Joseph included eunuchs, cupbearers, and bakers. Concerning these last two categories, there is no difficulty. Many kitchen offi- cials, brewers, bakers, and candymakers were in Pharaoh's service, and made bread and dainties for him, although we know next to nothing about the recipe for them. A special functionary stood behind Pharaoh when he ate. He was called either a *wdpw*, a word that can be translated "cupbearer," or *wba nsw*, "the king's valet." Among the aides that accompanied Ramses II on his expeditions, the man who carried a two-piece service made up of a water-

[2]"The Story of Si-nuhe," trans. John A. Wilson in James B. Pritchard, *ANET*, pp. 18-22.
[3]Adolf Erman, *AALA*, pp. 57-58.
[4]Papyrus Anastasi, III, VII, trans. in Pierre Montet, *DA*, p. 117.

Figure 11. A Royal Butler in the Country

bottle and a large goblet is undoubtedly a *wdpw* (fig. 11) .

On the other hand, the complete list of titles that can be found in Pharaoh's entourage does not provide us with a single word that can be translated "eunuch" *(saris)* and I strongly doubt that any such custom existed in the best known dynasties of the Old, Middle, or New Kingdoms and even of the Saïtic era. Could it be a practice peculiar to the court at Avaris? If so, it must have seemed a curious mixture of Asiatic and Egyptian customs. But such a conclusion must be allowed provisionally until texts give us further information on the question.

Another trait that is more Asiatic than Egyptian is the execution of the chief baker (Gen. 40:19) . Pharaoh, Joseph said to him, will have your head. He will hang you

⁵Harold H. Nelson and Uvo Hoelscher, *Medinet Habu: 1924–28* ("Oriental Institute Communications," No. 5 [Chicago: University of Chicago Press, 1929]) , pls. XXXVIII, LV. I have discovered the two pieces of this gold service in the tomb of Psusennes; cf. Pierre Montet, *Les constructions et le tombeau de Psoussenès*, Vol. II of *NRT*, Nos. 396-97.

Figure 12. A JAILED PRISONER

on a tree and the birds will eat the flesh off you. Pharaoh does, in fact, have him hung (Gen. 40:22). By "hung" we should probably understand "hung up," i.e., "impaled." The reader will be surprised to learn that we are very poorly informed about the way in which those who were condemned to death were executed. Those pictures which depict the king beating his enemies with a club, so common in the temples, can in no way be applied to those condemned under common law. The numerous papyri that refer to thefts from tombs enable us to be present at the inquiry during which suspects were beaten in different ways, but the penalties themselves have not come down to us. Condemnations to death were certainly pronounced after the plot against Ramses III, but we know only that they were carried out.[6] One of the stories from the Westcar papyrus gives us a glimpse of the fact

[6]Cf. A. De Buck, "The Judicial Papyrus of Turin," *JEA,* XXIII (1937), 152-64.

that a man condemned to death had his head cut off.[7] I do not believe that they were hung by the neck or impaled in the Syrian manner.

The word "rotunda," which is the word used for the prison in which the king's prisoners were kept (Gen. 39:20), does not have a known equivalent in Egyptian. A bas-relief recently discovered at Karnak shows a prisoner in jail (fig. 12). One cannot help thinking that Joseph may well have been lucky to leave the rotunda with his nose and ears still intact.[8]

When Pharaoh decided to put Joseph at the head of all Egypt he gave him his signet ring, put the gold chain around his neck, dressed him in fine linen garments, and had him ride in his second chariot (Gen. 41:42-43). Here the biblical narrative agrees with Egyptian texts and illustrated records. Nebunnef, for example, was invested with the dignity of first prophet of Amon in the following manner. Ramses II had already noted that Nebunnef had previously been neither second nor even fourth prophet, "and his majesty gave him his second gold ring and his gold cane. . . . A royal messenger was sent to all Egypt to let it be known that the house of Amon had been reconciled to him." [9]

During the Middle Kingdom men wore no other clothing than the loin cloth, but the custom of beautiful linen robes, for men as well as women, spread during the New Kingdom. In reward scenes, frequent during this era, Pharaoh threw necklaces and pectorals from the top of the Balcony of Appearances to officials who caught them and put them on the necks of those who were to be

[7]Cf. Papyrus Westcar, VIII: 13—IX, 1; cf. Lefebvre, *op. cit.*, p. 83.

[8]L. Keimer, "Das Bildauer Modell eines Mannes mit abgeschnittener Nase," *ZÄS*, LXXIX (1954), 140.

[9]G. Lefebvre, *Histoire des grands prêtres d'Amon de Karnak jusqu'à la XXIe dynastie* (Paris: P. Geuthner, 1929), p. 121.

Figure 13. PHARAOH REWARDS A PRISONER (LOUVRE C 213)

honored. Servants were allowed to pick up what was left over (fig. 13).[10]

The brave Ah-mose, who participated in combat when Avaris was capital, walked behind his lord who rode in a chariot.[11] But perhaps the kings of Avaris possessed a fleet of chariots before their Theban opponents, because it is well known that Egyptian words for horses, harness, and chariot parts have been borrowed from Semitic languages.[12] I cannot avoid concluding, however, that the

[10]Stele C 213 in the Louvre; cf. Norman de Garis Davies, *The Rock Tombs of El Amarna* (6 vols.; London, Boston: Egypt Exploration Fund, 1903–1908), I, pls. 25, 30; II, pls. 33, 37; III, pl. 16; IV, pl. 4; and *ibid., The Tomb of Nefer-hotep at Thebes* (New York: Metropolitan Museum of Art, 1933), pl. 14.

[11]*UAA*, IV, 3.

[12]Adolf Erman, *AALA*, pp. 615-16.

linen robes, horses, and chariots, as well as the mention
of the land of Ramses instead of Goshen, and the names
of such individuals as Zaphenath-paneah and Poti-Phera,
introduced by the Chronicler into the Joseph story, are
anachronisms. The picture which it presents of the Avaris
court includes more than one trait borrowed from the
Egypt of the time of Ramses II. The picture is nonetheless very valuable for Egyptologists who have at their disposal only a very small number of original documents for
the time of the Hyksos.

DREAMS

The king who welcomed Joseph, his cupbearer (butler),
and his baker are not the only known dreamers in Egypt.
Prince Thut-mose, who was not yet Thut-mose IV, fell
asleep in the shadow of the Sphinx while hunting. The
god appeared to him, complaining of being suffocated by
the sand, and promised the kingdom to him if he would
get rid of it for him. The prince obeyed and when he
became king, did not forget the dream that he had been
granted. In order to immortalize it, he had a stele engraved and placed between the paws of the monster; this
stele (the "Sphinx Stele") commemorates his first sand
removal.[13] Such a dream did not require an interpreter.
But the Ethiopian pharaoh, Ta-nut-Amon, felt extremely
perplexed one fine morning, and could not avoid relating
to his entourage what he had seen during the night: two
serpents, one to his right and the other to his left, who
disappeared immediately. The courtiers explained to him
that he already possessed Upper Egypt and that he was going to take Lower Egypt. Thus would the two goddesses

[13]"A Divine Oracle Through a Dream," in Pritchard, *op. cit.*, p. 449;
cf. also Gaston Maspéro, *Histoire de l'Orient: L'Egypte, Chaldéens et
Assyriens, les Israélites et les Phéniciens, les Mèdes et les Perses* (9 vols.;
Paris: Hachette, 1891), II, 294-95.

shine on his forehead, and the entire earth, without exception, would be his.[14]

Common people in Egypt also dreamed, and were absorbed with finding out what their dreams meant. In the New Kingdom a sort of dream key circulated which contained several divisions, each intended for a particular group of men: the followers of Horus, the followers of Seth, those who had a bad reputation, and perhaps others as well. The papyrus is not complete. The section concerning the followers of Horus is the only one that has come down to us intact.[15]

Often, the key to dreams worked by analogy. A good dream foretold a profit; a bad dream worry, great or small. If the dreamer received white bread he could count on pleasure. If he drank warm beer, it meant he would lose his goods. If he pricked himself with a thorn, lies would be told about him. If his fingernails were pulled out, he would be cheated out of his produce — a very common thing in ancient Egypt. If he dived into the Nile he would be cleansed of his sins.

Dreams about cows and ears of wheat and the cupbearer's dream are of this type. The baker's dream requires greater subtlety, however, just as certain dreams mentioned in the dream key were interpreted in unusual ways. Who would guess, for example, that to pilot a boat predicts the loss of a lawsuit?

The baker's dream inevitably augurs misfortune. Dreams in the key are on the whole warnings. If one knows how to go about it, he will escape the dire consequences that Seth inevitably sees in a bad dream. Pharaoh's dream is also a warning. Famine is in sight, but he depends on his governor's foresight to make it less formidable.

[14]"The Dream Stele, 4-6" in *UAA*, III, 62.
[15]Papyrus Chester Beatty, III. Cf. *Hieratic Papyri in the British Museum*, ed. A. H. Gardiner (3rd Ser.; London: British Museum, 1935), I, 9-23, II, pl. V–VIII; and Pritchard, *op. cit.*, p. 495.

WOMEN

Egyptian art gives a sympathetic, even moving, picture of the family; but literature is not fond of women — it accuses them of being frivolous, cruel, lying, and unfaithful. The Egyptian woman, Maspéro writes, never concerned herself with the fine points of sentiment. Sight of a handsome young man inspired in her nothing more nor less than physical passion, and her desire had to be satisfied on the spot.[16]

As a slave in the house of Potiphar, Joseph soon learned at great cost to himself to take account of the uninhibited behavior and treachery of Egyptian women (Gen. 39). An Egyptian tale, the Story of the Two Brothers (the manuscript of which dates to the time of Ramses II), provides us an example that is no less convincing.[17] "Lie with me," Potiphar's wife had said to Joseph. Likewise Anubis' wife said to her brother-in-law, Bata, "Come, let's spend an hour sleeping together! You won't regret it, because I shall make fine clothes for you."

The reaction of the two young men is just the same. "See here," says Bata, "you are like a mother to me and your husband is like a father to me." For Joseph adultery would be a sin against God. Moreover it would be a dreadful ingratitude to the man who refused him nothing of what was in his house except for his wife.

In the two cases the result is similar. Potiphar's wife and Anubis' wife attribute to Joseph and to Bata their guilty thoughts. As for the husbands, the one is just as easily duped as the other. Joseph was shut up in prison. Anubis' brother was less fortunate, for Anubis honed his knife to a razor sharp edge and hid behind the door to surprise him.

Could the Chronicler possibly have read or heard this

[16]Gaston Maspéro, *Les contes populaires de l'Egypte ancienne* (4th ed.; Paris: E. Guilmoto, 1911), XLIII.

[17]Pritchard, *op. cit.*, pp. 23-25.

Figure 14. The Swimmers' Patera

story with which all the scribes at Per-Ramses were undoubtedly familiar? There are many other guilty women in Egyptian stories but the story of Bata is the one which is the most nearly analogous to that of Joseph. To the Egyptian scribe it served as a prelude to the adventures which awaited the hero in the Valley of the Cedar. It fits perfectly into the Joseph story and undoubtedly those who heard or read it were completely happy to contrast the Egyptians' evil habits with the young Hebrew's purity.

Egyptologists feel that the story of Pharaoh's daughter, who went down to the Nile with her maids to bathe, is a highly unlikely one. Undoubtedly girls, whether they were princesses or not, learned how to swim at an early age (fig. 14) ,[18] but no princess needed to go down to the Nile and expose herself to indiscreet glances or a crocodile's attack. Undoubtedly the royal courtyard had pools within easy access.[19] But the princess had, of course, to see the cradle that contained the baby Moses.

The Hebrew midwives (Exod. 1:17) are not Egyptian women because their names, Shiphrah and Puah, are not Egyptian. However, in this passage mention of the double lying-in customary for women who were about to give birth makes one think of the story of Red-djedet who was delivered of her three children by three goddesses disguised as wandering musicians. Isis placed herself in front of the woman, Nephthys behind, and Hekat, the third, accelerated the birth process probably by massaging. Three times in succession a child slid into the hand of Isis, which makes us think that the patient had taken her place on a stool of a particular shape.[20]

---

[18]Swimmers are a frequently employed motif in the art of the New Kingdom. Examples include the wooden spoons in the Louvre, the swimmer's patera from the Wendebawended Cave (P. Montet, *NRT*, II, No. 775) , and the Tell Basta patera.

[19]The paintings in the tombs at Thebes prove that a pool was kept up near the dwelling.

[20]Lefebvre, *RCE*, pp. 86 ff.

THE BRICK CORVÉE

We have seen in a preceding chapter that slaves, some bought from merchants, the more numerous deported following a military expedition, were placed by the state at the disposal either of individuals or temples or in public services. The cleverest succeeded in earning the confidence of their masters (which is precisely what happened to Joseph), and in melting into the population mass, but the great majority and especially those who were employed in heavy construction were harshly treated. A bas-relief in the Bologne Museum shows a corvée of Negroes surrounded by scribes and soldiers. The scribes appear to be busy calling the role, while the soldiers are using their clubs or whips on these poor creatures (fig. 15).[21]

Figure 15. SCRIBES CALLING THE ROLL OF NEGROES SUBJECT TO FORCED LABOR
(BOLOGNE BAS-RELIEF)

Although the sons of Israel cannot be described as former prisoners of war, their condition was undoubtedly not much better after Pharaoh decided to use them as a group in brick-making and in the fields. They were supervised by foremen (Exod. 5:14) recruited from among the people of Israel and by taskmasters, their superiors,

[21]Erman, *op. cit.,* pl. XXXIX; F. W. von Bissing, *Denkmäler ägyptischer Sculptur* (Münich: F. Bruckmann, 1914), p. 81 A.

Figure 16. Brick Corvée

who were undoubtedly Egyptian since they beat the scribes when the daily quota was not met (Exod. 5:16).

A painting in the tomb of Rekh-mi-Re makes an excellent illustration of the biblical narrative. As a title it has "prisoners led by His Majesty for the construction of the temple of Amon who are making bricks to build once again the temple of Karnak."[22]

It must not be forgotten that the demand for rough bricks was enormous in ancient Egypt. Temples, tombs, and gateways to monuments were built of stone in order to merit their names as temples for millions of years or dwellings for eternity; but city walls, stores, schools, tax offices, private houses, and even royal palaces were of brick. Their walls were easily one meter thick; but the walls of towns were fifteen to eighteen meters thick and sufficiently high to hide everything inside, requiring truly formidable quantities of brick.

In fig. 16 workers have been placed near a body of water. Some are treading in a mixture of lime and chopped straw which had to be kept constantly warm, and others are stirring it with a mattock. When the mixture is ready,

[22]Norman de Garis Davies, *The Tomb of Rekh-mi-Rēʿ at Thebes* ("Publications of the Metropolitan Museum of Art," XI [New York: The Plantin Press, 1943]), pl. LVIII.

some of it is taken to the molders and replaced as often as necessary. A worker has just removed his mold and left a molded brick on the ground where it will dry quickly in the wind and sun. Once ready to use, the bricks are weighed on the two scales of a balance and carried to the foot of the wall being constructed. Foremen who have not forgotten their sticks move around in the middle of the work area.[23]

Of course the sons of Israel lamented the time they spent pasturing their flocks in the land of Goshen but their fate would have been much worse had it pleased Pharaoh to send them to pull stone blocks with the 'Apiru in the Bekhen mountains or in the Aswan quarries. They were at least able to stay with their wives and children.

WORK IN THE FIELDS

Although they were forced to make bricks, the sons of Israel were not free from working in the fields as well (Exod. 1:14). The Bible, however, does not say much about this particular activity except in one passage. In this passage the people who complain that they have been led out of Egypt are being persuaded that they have lost nothing in the exchange:

> "For the land which you are invading for conquest is not like the land of Egypt from which you came, where you used to sow your seed and water it by foot like a vegetable garden" (Deut. 11:10).

Had the Chronicler developed his thought he would have said that the Promised Land was watered by rain from the heavens, while in Egypt, even in the Delta, the rains were not sufficient to support vegetation. Water had to be brought up from underground through endless channels. From the time of the New Kingdom, Egyptians brought water up from underground with the help of a shaduf but in this work the foot played no part. We know

[23]*Ibid.*, pl. LIX.

of no elevator system which was operated by foot. Therefore I agree with the opinion of Edouard Dhorme, who
in commenting on this passage says that feet were used
to mark the ground with channels through which the ir-
rigating water flowed.

Seeding required of the Egyptian peasant far less effort
than what was needed in most ancient lands. As soon as
the land had "come out of" the water, to use the pictur-
esque expression of the author of the Story of Two
Brothers, seed was scattered and buried in the moist soil by
sending a herd over it, or, if the land had begun to dry
out, by using a mattock or plow.[24] Once that was done,
there was nothing to do until harvest time but to maintain and supply the irrigation canals.

FAMINE

The wealth and fertility of Egypt were proverbial
throughout all antiquity. In the desert the sons of Israel
thought more than once about the time when they allayed
their hunger by gathering around a cauldron. They said,
"O that we had flesh to eat! We remember the fish that
we used to eat for nothing in Egypt, the cucumbers, the
melons, the leeks, the onions and the garlic" (Num. 11:
4-5).

The Egyptians were assuredly great eaters of meat, especially of beef, fowl, and fish.[25] In certain nomes and
in certain families, it was no doubt forbidden to eat certain
kinds of fish or even all kinds;[26] but this prohibition was
far from being general. Fish from the Nile and the lakes
contributed largely to the food supply, especially of the
working classes. Fruits, salads, and vegetables made up the
rest of their diet. Watermelons are frequently depicted

[24]P. Montet, *Les Scènes de la vie privée dans les tombeaux égyptiens de
l'Ancien Empire* (Paris and Strasburg: Librairie Istra, 1925), pp. 183-92.
[25]*Ibid.*, p. 79.
[26]P. Montet, "Le fruit défendu," *Kêmi*, XI (1951), 85-116.

on Egyptian monuments.[27] Herodotus tells us that those
who worked on the pyramids ate onions in large quantities;[28] onions also appeared sometimes in the markets.[29]
I admit that garlic and leeks are not depicted and that we
are not sure of having identified their names, but the
witness of Herodotus and Dioscoridus corroborates the
biblical passage as far as garlic is concerned[30] and Pliny's
witness does the same for leeks. When the shipwrecked
sailor of the story arrived on his island, which he believed
to be deserted, he found there in profusion a good part
of what the sons of Israel missed so greatly: figs, grapes,
sycamore fruit, magnificent vegetables of all kinds, and
cucumbers that looked as if they had been cultivated, together with fish and birds.[31]

At the time of Joseph, however, this land was prey to
famine. The seven thin cows that devoured the seven fat
cows and the seven withered ears that utterly destroyed
as many good ears announced seven years of want during
which the resources they had accumulated during the preceding seven years of abundance would disappear.

A stele discovered in 1889 on the island of Sehel[32] at
the tip of Egypt was immediately interpreted by the
Egyptologist Brugsch as an Egyptian version of the biblical
narrative.[33] In the eighteenth year of King Djoser, the
builder of the Step Pyramid, and thus at the beginning
of the history of the pharaohs, the Nile had not flooded
on time for a period of seven years. Grain was not very

[27]L. Keimer, *Die Gartenpflanzen im alten Ägypten: ägyptologische
Studien* (Hamburg: Hoffmann und Campe, 1924), pp. 13-18, 171.
[28]Herodotus, II, 125.
[29]Scene from the *mastaba* of Ptah-Shepses at Abusir.
[30]Cf. Victor Loret, "L'ail chez les anciens Egyptiens," *Sphinx*, VIII
(1904), 137-47.
[31]Cf. Naufragé 47-53 in Lefebvre, *op. cit.*, p. 34.
[32]Paul Barguet, *La stèle de la famine à Sehel* (Cairo: Imprimerie de
l'Institut français d'archéologie orientale, 1953).
[33]H. K. Brugsch, *Die biblischen sieben Jahre der Hungersnoth nach dem
Wortlaut einer altägyptischen Felsen-inschrift* (Leipzig: J. C. Hinrichs,
1891).

abundant and ears withered. Everything available for eating was in short supply. Everyone was cheated out of his income; the hearts of the old men were heavy; and even members of the royal court were in need and temples were shut.

In these unfavorable circumstances Pharaoh saw fit to question a wise man, one of Im-hotep's priests, who went to the town of Thoth to unroll the sacred books. He came back with interesting revelations. The king made a complete offering to the gods and goddesses of Elephantine and then while he was sleeping, Khnum, the god of the cataract, appeared to him and announced that he would cause the Nile to rise and there would no longer be an inadequate flooding in the future.

The terms and the scope of the dream (which on the stele follows rather than precedes the famine), the explanations of the wise man and the outcome of the event are not like the biblical account. It could nevertheless be admitted that the Chronicler borrowed the seven years of famine, the intervention of a wise man and Pharaoh's dream from an Egyptian legend, if we could be sure that the stele comes from a time prior to the era of the king of Avaris. No one believes any longer, since Maspéro,[34] that the stele was engraved in the days of Djoser. It was rather a pious lie conceived much later to draw the king's favor to the sanctuary at Khnum. Some modern commentators reject the idea of a forgery and date the stele either in the time of Ptolemy X,[35] or of Ptolemy V.[36] If this is correct, we can no longer hold that the Chronicler remembered an Egyptian legend. It would, on the contrary, be the priests of Khnum who would have known

---

[34]Maspéro, *Histoire*, I, 239-42.

[35]Kurt Sethe, *Dodekaschoinos, das Zwölfmeilen land an der Grenze von Ägypten und Nubien*, Vol. II of *Untersuchungen zur Geschichte und Altertumskunde Ägyptens* (Leipzig: J. C. Hinrichs, 1901), p. 75.

[36]Barguet, *op. cit.*, p. 33.

the Joseph story through the Jews of Elephantine.[37] This conclusion is in no way necessary, however. Sethe, who dates the stele in the time of Ptolemy X, is forced to show that his editors had used and modernized a very ancient document, dating possibly from the time of Djoser.[38] Barguet recalls that in countries other than Egypt, the tradition of a seven year famine is attested.[39] What Maspéro has so well said about popular stories can be extended to this tradition: "If Egypt was not their land of origin, it was there that these stories became naturalized in the distant past and took literary form." [40]

In this land of abundance, the specter of famine could never be forgotten. Harvests depended on flooding and a wide distribution of the Nile's waters. Too great a flooding was almost as disastrous as too small a flooding. A few canals that had not been dredged could easily wipe out the harvest of a whole province. Greek and Arab texts report appalling famines. Egyptian antiquity, too, knew of more than one, especially in troubled times.[41]

A priest named Heqa-nakht, who lived during one of these periods, wrote to his family:

> Behold, you are like a man who once ate as much as he wanted and now is hungry up to the very time he closes his eyes. I have arrived in the South and I have gathered for you the largest possible number of victuals . . . Is the Nile not very low? . . . Why, they have begun to eat men and women here! Nowhere else in the world have there existed people who have been given such food.[42]

[37]Jacques Vandier, *La famine dans l'Egypte ancienne* (Cairo: Imprimerie de l'Institut français d'archéologie orientale, 1936), pp. 40-44.

[38]In the majority of the large temples, an establishment existed called the "house of life" which was a sort of conservatory for traditions; cf. A. H. Gardiner, "The House of Life," *JEA*, XXIV (1938), 157, and Serge Sauneron, *Les prêtres de l'ancienne Egypte* (Paris: Editions du Seuil, 1957), p. 133. That is why many texts from the Ptolemaic temples were written in the style of ancient rituals.

[39]Barguet, *op. cit.*, p. 37.   [40]Maspéro, *CP*, pl. LXXII.   [41]Vandier, *op. cit.*

[42]Cf. the letter translated by Battiscombe Gunn in the *Bulletin of the Metropolitan Museum of Art*, XVII, Part II (1922), 37 ff.; and Vandier, *op. cit.*, pp. 13-14.

A governor of one of the provinces, Ankh-tifi, somewhat earlier gave a testimony of the same kind: "The whole of Upper Egypt died of starvation to the point where each man was even eating his own children." [43]

The civil war called the War of the Unclean which exploded during the last years of the XX dynasty brought about an unbelievably severe famine. A woman questioned at court on the source of her money, answered: "I got it in exchange for wheat in the year of the hyenas when everyone was hungry . . ." [44] So many people probably died that year that no one had time to even bury the dead, with the result that the hyenas came and devoured them in the towns and villages.

Joseph's information would not, therefore, surprise the Pharaoh of Avaris who set aside one-fifth of the harvest during the seven years of abundance (Gen. 41:34-35). When the famine spread over the whole land, Joseph opened the depots and sold wheat to Egypt (Gen. 41:56).

The governors of the nomes did not operate any differently when a low Nile made it possible to foresee a meager harvest. Here, for example, is what Ankh-tifi did:

> . . . I had this grain rushed from the south. It arrived at the land of Wawat in the south and the Great Land in the north . . . I granted a grain loan to Upper Egypt and I gave some to the north. I enabled the house of Elephantine to live; I enabled Ox Hill to live during those years, after Hefat and Hor-mer had been satisfied. [45]

Not only did Ankh-tifi and his rivals distribute grain to all those under their jurisdiction, but these good gov-

---

[43]Jacques Vandier, *Mo'alla: la tombe d'Ankhtifi et la tombe de Sébekhotep* (Cairo: Imprimerie de l'Institut français d' archéologie orientale, 1950), pp. 210-13; this is inscription 10 from Ankh-tifi's tomb.
[44]Papyrus 10052 in the British Museum as translated in T. Eric Peet, *The Great Tomb Robberies of the Twentieth Egyptian Dynasty* (Oxford: Clarendon Press, 1930), pp. 152-53.
[45]Vandier, *Mo'alla* . . . , pp. 210ff. Ankh-tifi lived at Hefat, and Hor-mer was located nearby.

ernors did not take advantage of the situation in order to line their own pockets. The following examples illustrate this point:

> I have not taken a man's daughter from him, nor have I taken his field.[46]

> When a low Nile occurred in the year XXV, I did not leave my nome hungry. I gave southern wheat and barley to the people. I did not let want occur before the great Niles had returned.[47]

> When years of famine struck I had every field in the nome tilled . . . In those years when the Niles, mistresses of wheat, barley and all good things, were plentiful I wrote nothing on the tax accounts.[48]

But Joseph, foreign minister to a foreign king, does not hide the fact that he was following quite another policy (Gen. 47:14). At first he had all the money that was to be found in Egypt and the land of Canaan brought into the house of Pharaoh.[49] When there was no money left, he took the flocks of large and small livestock (Gen. 47: 17). When the flocks were exhausted, he took land with the exception of that which belonged to the priests which he could not acquire because a decree by Pharaoh had declared it inalienable. Then he transferred those who lived in the country to the towns.

It is true that temple property could not be confiscated by the state; we possess a whole series of decrees protecting the personnel and goods of the temples against the

---

[46]Stele 20001 from Cairo; cf. Vandier, *op. cit.*, p. 106.
[47]Inscription of Ameni at Beni Hasan; cf. *Beni Hasan,* ed. Percy E. Newberry (4 vols.; London: K. Paul, Trench, Trübner and Co., 1893–1900), I, pl. VIII, 1, 19; and Vandier, *op. cit.*
[48]Stele of a Mentu-hotep; cf. Vandier, *op. cit.*, p. 113.
[49]The authority of the king of Avaris, ruler over a large section of Egypt, probably extended to the land of Canaan. It was, moreover, bound by a close alliance with the lord of Retenu; cf. *Comptes Rendus de l'Académie des Inscriptions et Belles-Lettres* (Paris: Imprimerie Nationale, 1956), 158.

excessive zeal of civil servants.[50] As for the transactions effected by Joseph, they were undoubtedly more theoretical than factual since it was impossible to remove farmers from their fields. In what follows in Genesis 47 we learn that Joseph appropriated only one-fifth of the harvest— still a large amount, of course, and enough to justify Ka-mose's claim that the Egyptians had been crushed by taxes under the Asians.[51]

[50]For the Old Kingdom, cf. the decrees of Coptos and Memphis in *UAA*, I, 274-307. For the New Kingdom see the inscription of Radesieh in *Recueil de travaux relatifs à la philologie et à l'archéologie égyptiennes et assyriennes*, XIII (1885?), 75, and the inscription of Nauri in *JEA*, XIII (1927), 193.

[51]Cf. the Carnavon Tablet, I, 4, in *JEA*, III (1916), 38-39.

6

Magic and Superstition

AARON'S SERPENT

For the common people magic was a means of defense against illness, accident, bad omens, and enemies. It gave formulas against every evil — from preventing the robbery of kites [birds] to making the hair of a rival fall out.[1] The kind of magic passed on by storytellers was more ambitious. The Westcar papyrus knows of magicians capable of replacing decapitated heads, of relocating lost objects by placing one half of a container of lake water on the other, and changing wax crocodiles into real crocodiles that would get hold of a culprit and drag him to the bottom of the lake.[2] This was only child's play, however, compared to the powers that the reading of a book written by the hand of Thoth would confer:

> If you recite the first formula you will enchant heaven, earth, the world of the night, the mountains and bodies of water; you will understand what the birds of the heavens and reptiles are saying, as long as they live . . . If you read the second formula, while you are yet in your grave you will resume the form that you had while you were on earth.[3]

[1]P. Montet, *VQ*, p. 75.
[2]Gustave Lefebvre, *RCE*, pp. 74-76.
[3]Cf. the demotic history of Setna-Kha-monwas in Gaston Maspéro, *CP*, p. 108.

Just as scribes and civil servants questioned the ability of their colleagues to erect obelisks, build dikes, or organize expeditions abroad,[4] so magicians flung maledictions at each other. The competition was far more interesting, however, if it put a foreigner into conflict with an Egyptian. A pesky Ethiopian presented himself one day at the palace of the pharaoh with a secret message, stating that if no one was able to read it, it would be taken for granted that Egypt was inferior to Ethiopia.[5] One night an Ethiopian sorcerer by a magic spell seized a pharaoh and carried him to his homeland where he gave him 500 lashes with a kourbash. He was all ready to repeat the whipping when, fortunately for the pharaoh, an Egyptian magician went to Thoth's temple and not only prevented the Ethiopian from renewing his dastardly deed but also seized the king of the Negroes and inflicted on him an equivalent punishment.[6]

At the beginning of the conflict between the sons of Israel and Egypt's pharaoh, Aaron and the Egyptian magicians pitted wits against each other. When Aaron changed a staff into a serpent, the Pharaoh called his wise men and his sorcerers who did the same thing by means of their occult wisdom, but Aaron's staff swallowed up theirs (Exod. 7:11-12).

This miracle was quite capable of making the Pharaoh's mind perplexed and fearful. Serpents were justly feared throughout all Egypt. The large snakes who in prehistoric times had attacked elephants and lions had disappeared, but the tiny viper and the dreaded cobra continued to

[4]Cf. Papyrus Anastasi, I, in A. H. Gardiner, *Literary Texts of the New Kingdom*, Ser. I of *Egyptian Hieratic Texts* (Leipzig: J. C. Hinrichs, 1911), pp. 14-30.
[5]Cf. the second demotic history of Setna and his son in Maspéro, *CP*, p. 139. The son was also able to show his father that the wicked rich man and the good man deprived of everything were treated in Amenti (the Other World) according to their merits; cf. Pierre Montet, *Eternal Egypt* (London: Weidenfeld and Nicolson, 1964), p. 184.
[6]Maspéro, *CP*, pp. 143 ff.

kill many. How could they defend themselves against such enemies except by magic? Amulets representing the child Horus standing on crocodiles holding scorpions and serpents in his hands were thought to be quite effective. Repetition of the words of the gods who had triumphed over these animals was considered advantageous. Holy men who had acquired a wide reputation for protecting their fellow citizens by curing those who had been bitten came to be regarded as of use even after their deaths. One of them named Djed-her, for example, gave his statue, which he had placed on a pedestal, to the temple in his town where it was set in front of a small fountain.[7] Proven formulas were engraved on the clothing or even on the flesh. The faithful drew water, spread it on the holy man, and then drank it after it had supposedly become imbued with the efficacy of the formulas.

Djed-her and those like him made their living very much like those snake charmers of very recent times so well studied by L. Keimer.[8] They did not have the ability to change a staff into a serpent, but it was a simple matter for them to change a serpent into a staff, that is, to make it as stiff as a staff, and at the end of a certain period of time to give it back its ability to move and to harm. On a scarab from Tanis, I believe I can recognize a magician doing his tricks before a divine trio (fig. 17).[9] Many scarabs are illustrated with a scene of the same type: a man or god holds in his fist a snake straight as a staff.[10] Temple bas-reliefs that have as their title "the striking of calves"

[7]Pierre Lacau, *Les statues "guerisseuses" de l'ancienne Egypte*, Vol. XXV in *Monuments et Mémoires publiés par l' Académie des Inscriptions et Belles-lettres, Commission de la fondation Piot* (Paris: Ernest Leroux, 1921–1922).

[8]L. Keimer, *Histoires de serpents dans l'Egypte ancienne et moderne*, Vol. L of *Mémoires de l'Institut d'Egypte* (Cairo: Imprimerie de l'Institut français d'archéologie orientale, 1947).

[9]P. Montet, *Tanis: Douze années de fouilles dans une capitale oubliée du delta égyptien* (Paris: Payot, 1942), p. 219 (fig. 63).

[10]Keimer, *op. cit.*, p. 19.

Figure 17. SNAKE CHARMER BEFORE THE GODS (TANIS SCARAB)

could also be mentioned. The man who is driving four calves of different colors in front of him has a staff in his hand that ends in a snake's head (fig. 18).[11] A magician who was supposed to seize a small chest found it guarded by serpents, scorpions, and reptiles, but he rendered them motionless.[12]

These texts and figures are largely from a later period but that does not mean these superstitions or customs arose only in the later period. They come from all periods, and the Chronicler was acquainted with these practices when he wrote the episode of Aaron and the serpents.

THE EGYPTIAN PLAGUES

Aaron's snake was only a prelude. Pharaoh was hard-hearted and it was necessary to inflict upon him even greater signs which, however, did not have much more success. These were the ten plagues.

The first plague, water changed into blood, makes us think of an innocuous phenomenon that occurs during

[11]A. M. Blackmann and H. W. Fairman, "The Significance of the Ceremony *Ḥwt Bḥsw* [The Striking of Calves] in the Temple of Horus at Edfu," *JEA*, XXXV (1949), 98-112.
[12]Cf. Setna in Maspéro, *op. cit.*, p. 112.

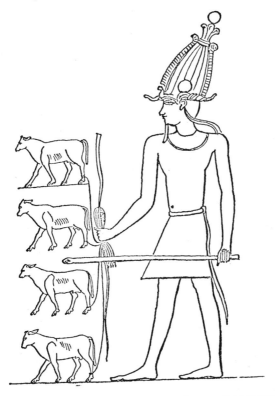

Figure 18. THE KING DRIVING CALVES WITH A SERPENT-BECOME-STAFF

flooding, when waves first stir the waters which have remained in the swamps from preceding years. This is the
"green Nile" which causes bladder trouble. Once the
water has been filtered in a simple *zir*, however, it can be
drunk without hesitation. After the green Nile comes the
red Nile. The color is so intense, Maspéro writes,[13] that
at certain times it looks like a flow of freshly shed blood.
The red Nile is not injurious and loses its color when
gently poured. But the red Nile probably has nothing to

[13]Gaston Maspéro, *Histoire de l'Orient: l'Egypte, Chaldéens et Assyriens,
les Israélites et les Phéniciens, les Mèdes et les Perses* (9 vols.; Paris:
Hachette, 1891), I, 23.

do with the first plague that the Egyptian magicians reproduced in their turn through their occult wisdom (Exod. 7:22), since the changing of water into blood is a magic motif that appears in Egypt itself: "If I am defeated," a magician says to his mother to warn her, "when you eat or drink, the water that you drink will become the color of blood before you and the sky will become the color of blood in front of you."[14] It may perhaps be objected that the story of Setu is known to us through a papyrus from the time of the Ptolemies; nevertheless the person and the situations belong to the New Kingdom. The Chronicler could have been familiar with it or heard an analogous story in which the red color of the water or sky, Seth's color, forecast disastrous happenings.

Frogs, mosquitoes, and gnats make up the second, third, and fourth plagues. Frogs in small numbers sometimes appear among the innumerable denizens of swamps.[15] Its name *qrr (ḳrr)* is onomatopoetic.[16] Amulets exist in the form of frogs.[17] The god Khnum had as his consort a goddess with the head of a frog who came to the help of women in labor.[18] Nothing in all this is surprising; if, however, at some point frogs multiplied to the point of being a plague, the Egyptians have not recorded the fact.

Small insects (fleas, aphids, lice, mosquitoes, and gnats) abound in Egypt and are extremely troublesome. Egyptians have long sought to guard against them. To keep them from the noble faces of the king and lords, servants

[14]Gaston Maspéro, *CP*, p. 150.

[15]Cf. F. W. von Bissing, *Die Mastaba des Gem-ni-kai* (2 vols.; Berlin; Alexander Duncker, 1905–1911), I, pl. IV.

[16]*WAS*, ed. A. Erman and H. Grapow, V, 61. This word is vocalized *ḳrur* like the Babylonian proper name Pakruru.

[17]P. Montet, *BE*, Nos. 448, 449.

[18]His temple was located in the XVth nome of Upper Egypt; cf. Gustave Lefebvre, *Le tombeau de Petosiris* (3 vols.; Cairo: Imprimerie de l'Institut français d'archéologie orientale, 1923–1924), II, inscriptions 61 and 81; cf. also Ridolfo V. Lanzone, *Dizionario di Mitologia Egizia* (6 vols.; Turin: Litografia Fratelli Doyen, 1881–1886), II, 852.

would wave ostrich plumes on the end of a stick.[19] Medical papyri recommend several means of ridding the house of mosquitoes. Floors and walls were washed with a solution of soda. Cat grease was said to be effective against rats, fish spawn against fleas. Egyptians dressed in linen, because they feared woolen clothes for themselves as well as for the dead.[20] They took great care of their bodies, washed, depilated, and massaged several times a day. They were not ignorant of the fact that nomads were covered with lice and that they even ate them.[21]

Locusts, the eighth plague, were without a doubt a curse to the farmer. The author of the satire on trades does not forget them when he enumerates the calamities which prevented peasants from being paid for their work. They often wore amulets in the form of locusts and begged a locust god to keep his subjects away from their crops.[22]

Let us now pass to murrain (the fifth plague) and children's contagious diseases (the tenth plague). Egyptian texts make no references to the former. However, monarchs, in the inscriptions on their tombs, do not fail to mention the efforts that they made to improve livestock. Entire herds were brought in from the south and from Lybia.[23] On at least two occasions, Syrian cattle were sent to Egypt.[24] These repeated efforts can only be explained by saying that murrain periodically devastated the flocks of the Nile Valley.

A medical tract indicates the means of distinguishing

[19]Adolf Erman, *AALA*, p. 69.
[20]Si-nuhe, B 199; cf. Gustave Lefebvre, *RCE*, p. 17.
[21]P. Montet, *VQ*, p. 73.
[22]Ludwig Keimer, "Pendeloques en forme d'insectes faisant partie de colliers égyptiens," *ASAE*, XXXIII (1933), 100-130, 193-200; cf. the whole bibliography of Ricardo A. Caminos, *Late Egyptian Miscellanies* (London: Oxford University Press, 1954), p. 248.
[23]P. Montet, "Les boeufs égyptiens," *Kêmi*, XIII (1954), 43.
[24]Once from Megiddo by Thut-hotep; cf. Aylward M. Blackmann, "An Indirect Reference to Sesostris III's Syrian Campaign in the Tomb-Chapel of DḤWTY-ḤTP at El-Bersheh," *JEA*, II (1915), 13-14. On another occasion under Thut-mose III; cf. *UAA*, IV, 664.

the child likely to live from one doomed to die. If he says *Ni* he will live; but if he utters a cry like the moaning of the wind in a pine forest, he will die.[25] On another occasion a mother leaning over a child who was close to death tried to ward off that enemy by chanting:

Did you come to kiss this child?
I will not let you kiss it.
Did you come to put it to sleep?
I will not let you put it asleep.
Did you come to take it away?
I will not allow you to take it away from me.

Many children undoubtedly died at an early age in ancient Egypt. During excavations at Tanis, an epidemic killed about fifty children in two or three weeks.[26]

Medical tracts also draw attention to a disease that can be compared to boils, the sixth plague.[27] And in conclusion, hail (the seventh plague) and darkness (the ninth plague) are two natural phenomena. Small hailstones frequently fall in the north of the Delta during the winter, causing only minor damage. I remember that once, on May 15, 1945, after a stifling heatwave, hailstones as large as walnuts fell for more than five minutes, cutting crops to shreds and injuring man and beast alike. In 1930 I noticed a huge coal-black cloud forming. When it was over us, a very short while later, the whole country was plunged into darkness and it could have been said that someone had dumped unbelievable quantities of dust onto the earth from the sky. The phenomenon lasted twenty minutes and the weather did not become normal again until about two days had passed. Every year, too,

[25] Papyrus Ebers, No. 838.
[26] Cf. Zauberspruche, I:9-II:6 in Gustave Lefebvre, *Essai sur la medecine égyptienne de l'époque pharaonique* (Paris: Presses universitaires de France, 1956), p. 113.
[27] *Ibid.*, p. 193-94; Deuteronomy 28:27 warns the one who will not listen to the voice of Yahweh that his God will smite him with Egyptian sores, with ulcers, scurvy, and an incurable itch.

Plate VIII. Foundation Sacrifice in a Tanis Wall

99

the *khamsin* wind rages with greater or lesser violence several times throughout the spring season.

The Egyptian plagues can therefore pass as a summary of the calamities or annoyances that strike the inhabitants of the eastern Delta without the slightest supernatural intervention. It had been this way "since the time of the god," and it would be quite natural to think that these phenomena were caused by some malevolent deity and that a magician who was sufficiently trained in his art could reproduce them at will. Thus when the king of the Negroes was taking an afternoon nap, an Ethiopian magician suggested casting a spell on Egypt to force the Egyptian people to spend three days and three nights without seeing any daylight following the darkness.[28] If no allusion is made to other kinds of plagues in the stories in which the magician appears, it is probably quite accidental. The Chronicler has merely attributed to Moses tricks analogous to those that were common among Egyptian magicians.

FOUNDATION SACRIFICES

Leviticus forbids anyone to cause one of his children to pass through the fire to Moloch; and the prophets were indignant with this custom, an everyday occurrence in the land of Canaan where it is attested by both archaeology and literary texts.

When Joshua took Jericho, he had an oath pronounced against it, saying:

"Cursed be the man before the Lord,
Who undertakes to rebuild this city, Jericho;
At the cost of his first-born shall he lay its
    foundation,
And at the cost of his youngest
    son shall he erect its gates" (Josh. 6:26).

This prophecy was fulfilled when Hiel of Bethel rebuilt Jericho. He laid its foundation at the cost of his firstborn,

[28]Maspéro, *CP*, p. 143.

100

Abiram, and he set up its gates at the cost of his youngest son Segub (I Kings 16:34). The Tanis mission was greatly surprised to find that the Egyptians themselves had practiced this custom that one would think would be unknown in the Nile Valley.

The great wall of Tanis which had been repaired more than once is certainly not a homogeneous construction, but it has been definitely established that the north wall goes back to a time prior to the reign of Psusennes. It could even have been built at the time of Ramses the Great. In 1929 while this wall was being cleared away to the approaches of the north gate, a skeleton lying in the sand one meter from the corner came into view; and a bit farther along a large cigar-shaped jar of baked earth was discovered, containing a second skeleton, that of an infant.[29] Two years later we found the same phenomenon in the recess in the north gate, the skeleton of an adult or of a tall boy lying in the sand, and the skeleton of a child in a jar (pl. VIII).[30] This barbarous custom continued at Tanis after the War of the Unclean and the triumph of Amon. When Psusennes had the wall built, all of whose bricks are stamped with his name, two jars containing a child's skeleton were placed in it, one in the recess in the east gate and the other on the outside of this gate. A fifth jar, which is perhaps more recent, was found in the Temple of the East.[31]

Outside of Tanis foundation sacrifice existed only in the Wadi Tumilat, through which travelers from Palestine to Egypt would pass.[32] Archaeologists have also verified its practice in the land of Canaan at Megiddo, Taan-

[29]P. Montet, *NFT*.

[30]Cf. *Kêmi*, V (1935), pls. IV and IX.

[31]The jar placed on the outside of the East Gate and the one found in the Temple of the East were discovered in 1947.

[32]W. M. F. Petrie, *Hyksos and Israelite Cities* (London: School of Archaeology, University College, 1906), pp. 22, 29.

ach, and Gezer.[33] In spite of the indignant protestations of the prophets, Israelites who had settled in Palestine both sacrificed children and placed their bodies in foundations.[34] This custom was thus borrowed by the Egyptians from the Semites, since it is only found in places in Egypt frequented by Semites.

FORBIDDEN THINGS

The idea of forbidden fruit is very ancient and very important in the Egypt of the time of the pharaohs.[35] Each nome, each town even, had those taboos which were peculiar to it and through which it distinguished itself from its neighbors. These taboos usually concerned animals, mammals, birds, and fish that could neither be captured, eaten, or even touched because the local god took certain kinds under his protection—for example, the hippopotamus in the tenth nome of Upper Egypt; or, on the other hand, because he reserved to himself the right to hunt and kill it—the hippopotamus again in the nome of Edfu. Sometimes it was sufficient to prohibit only part of the body, that part offered to the god. Sometimes, also, it was an inanimate thing that was taboo; gold, for example, was taboo in one town of the twelfth nome of Upper Egypt because the local god, the ferryman of his state, had allowed himself to be corrupted by a small amount of gold. These taboos and also those which concerned certain actions were not therefore inspired by hygienics or morality as were those which appear in Deuteronomy 14. Nevertheless people did not take them lightly.[36] Brawls

[33]Adolphe Lods, *Israël, dès origines au milieu du VIIIe siècle* (Paris: La Renaissance du Livre, 1930) , pp. 113-14.

[34]*Ibid.*, pp. 328-29.

[35]P. Montet, "Le fruit défendu," *Kêmi, XI* (1951) , 85.

[36]Thus for Israel the pig, which has cloven hoofs but does not chew its cud, was unclean (Deut. 14:8) . In Egypt the pig is unclean because Horus had become blind while looking at a black pig, or rather at Seth who had taken this form. The gods decided that the pig was taboo for Horus and all those faithful to him.

and even bloody battles took place because the inhabitants of one town invaded that of their neighbors and killed or ate animals that were to be spared.[37]

This intolerance was certainly familiar to Moses, and that is why he required Pharaoh to let the sons of Israel go a three days' journey into the desert to make sacrifices to Yahweh. They were afraid of being stoned by the Egyptians if they were to make a sacrifice that was abhorrent to them (Exod. 8:26-27).[38] This was not an unrealistic fear. The Jews of Elephantine would learn this to their own misfortune at the end of the fifth century. If the inhabitants of the cataract finally destroyed the temple of Yaho, it is undoubtedly because revolt against Persian domination was brewing in the land and Jewish mercenaries of the king of kings were being forced to fight it; but it was also because the Jews sacrificed the paschal lamb in a land that had the ram-god Khnum, the native protector of all kinds of sheep, as its deity.[39]

It was even forbidden for Egyptians to take their meals in the company of those who did not practice the same taboos. Genesis 43:32 is to be explained in this way; there it is said that Joseph was served apart from his brothers because Egyptians could not associate with Hebrews. When Pi-ankhi had conquered all Upper Egypt and a part of Lower Egypt he did not want to authorize the conquered princes to go into the royal palaces because they were not circumcised and ate fish. Only Nemarot was received in the palace because he was pure and did not eat fish.[40] After a historical text let us mention a passage

[37]Cf. Plutarch, *On Isis and Osiris,* 72.

[38]In the Eastern Harpoon whose capital was Pithom, the foreleg was a forbidden thing. The royal house of Per-Ramses certainly had a list of taboos; an inscription of Ramses IV gives us an idea of what they were like; cf. P. Montet, "Le fruit . . .", *Kêmi,* XI (1951), 109.

[39]Albert Vincent, *La religion des Judéo-Araméens d'Eléphantine* (Paris: P. Geuthner, 1937).

[40]Cf. Pi-ankhi, 150-52 in *UAA,* III, 54.

from a story. When the envoy of the Ethiopians came to the palace of the pharaoh to provoke the Egyptians, he did not receive his answer until ten days had passed. He was assigned rooms where he was to remain, and unclean foods were prepared for him according to Ethiopian customs.[41] Such touchiness became even more extreme when relations were strained.

[41]Maspéro, *CP*, p. 140.

7

Piety and Morality

GOD

Did the Hebrews realize the splendor of Egyptian monuments? Many have wondered if the complex created by Solomon (including the temple to Yahweh, the king's palace, and the House of the Forest of Lebanon) did not reproduce in its basic format an Egyptian village with its wall, monumental gates, temple, and palace, the front of which faced on the courtyard of the temple. It is possible that the columns with their capitals in the form of lilies imitated the floral columns of the Egyptians. But no answer can be given to these questions. Unfortunately the description of the temple in the first book of Kings does not take the place of either the disappeared remains or an illustrated document.

The Bible mentions Egyptian monuments only to announce their approaching destruction by fire (Jer. 43:13), the punishment of Amon of No (Thebes) (Jer. 46:25), and the destruction of Noph (Memphis) that Yahweh would erase from the very memory of man (Ezek. 30:13). Thus the piety of the Egyptians, regarded by Herodotus as the most religious of men,[1] does not seem to have impressed Israel's wise men. It might be said that the only

[1] Herodotus, II, 37.

thing they remembered was what Deuteronomy 29:17 calls their "detestable" and horrid "idols." There were, however, many common points between Egyptian piety and morality and their own. We are going to try in this last chapter to shed some light on these similarities and see if they cannot be explained by the repeated and prolonged contacts that the two people had with each other.

On the surface, nothing could be more different than their religious ideas. Israel had a national God that the great prophets transformed into a universal God. The Egyptians peopled the universe with a multitude of gods in strange, monstrous, and grotesque forms which scandalized Greeks and Romans. None of these gods succeeded in supplanting the others, despite some attempts. The disk with the rays that end in hands is treated in the Tell el-Amarna hymns as a unique god who created the heavens and the earth and called beings by the thousands into existence, but it has not been established that the promulgation of a new doctrine so passionately supported by the king was enough to put an end to polytheism. The latter soon recovered all its strength. Ramses III portioned out his wealth to three principle gods: Amon of Thebes, Ptah of Memphis, and Atum of Onu, but he did not forget the less important powers firmly rooted in Nebi, Coptos, This, Abydos, Khmunu, and Siut; nor even the gods of little renown who also received personnel, livestock, lands, and commodities.[2]

It is nonetheless true that the Bible sometimes places ideas worthy of the great prophets in the mouth of Pharaoh. Thus in Genesis 41:38-39, Pharaoh, astonished by Joseph's explanations, says to his servants, "Can we find a man with the spirit of God (Elohim) in him like this one?" Then Pharaoh said to Joseph, "Since God has made

---

[2]This distribution is the object of Papyrus Harris, I; cf. W. Erichsen, *Papyrus Harris I: Hieroglyphische Transkription,* Vol. V in BA.

all this known to you, there is no one so shrewd and prudent as you." The Hyksos king was not referring to the god of Avaris, Seth, for whom he professed such an exclusive devotion that he dreamt of imposing his worship on all Egypt. Would the Chronicler have made an improper usage of the word "God"? Certainly not; such a usage is well attested in ancient Egypt. A religious text from the Middle Kingdom speaks of the god that exists in man.[3] The pious Pahery, governor of el-Kab at the beginning of the XVIII dynasty prided himself on knowing the god who is in men.[4] A manager of storehouses placed god in his heart and resorted to his power.[5] Such examples prove that the Chronicler has Pharaoh speak in Genesis 40 like a true Egyptian and that he has not bestowed the Hebrew tongue on him in any way.

The use of the word *ntjr* (God) in its most general sense at times when the name of a particular god could be expected is in fact very common and is met in every epoch—first in the collections of maxims under the Old Kingdom in the Plan of Men for Ka'gemni,[6] in the maxims of Ptah-hotep,[7] in the Middle Kingdom in the instruction for Meri-ka-Re,[8] in the New Kingdom in the instruction of Ani,[9] and also in stelae of particular individuals in which praise of the deceased unfortunately takes up more space than does factual narrative. We are

[3]Adolf Erman, *La religion des Egyptiens,* trans. Henri Wild (Paris: Payot, 1937), p. 194, n. 6.
[4]*UAA,* IV, 119.
[5]The Turin Stele, No. 156; cf. Alexandre Varille, "La stèle du mystique Béky," *Bulletin de l'Institut français d'archéologie orientale du Caire,* LIV (1954), 129.
[6]The ending of this book occupies the last two pages of Papyrus Prisse.
[7]Cf. James B. Pritchard, *ANET,* pp. 412-14; Eugène Dévaud, *Les maximes de Ptah-hotep* (Fribourg: Imprimerie de l'Oeuvre de Saint-Paul, 1916) (text only); and Adolf Erman, *The Literature of the Ancient Egyptians* (London: Methuen and Co., Ltd., 1927), pp. 54-66.
[8]Cf. the Ermitage (Leningrad) Papyrus 1116A as translated in Pritchard, *op. cit.,* pp. 414-18; and commentary of Alexander Scharff, *Der historische Abschnitt der Lehre für König Merikarê* (Munich: C. H. Beck, 1936).
[9]Cf. Pritchard, *ANET,* pp. 420-21.

repeatedly told that God knows everything, that he can do anything, that no one knows his purposes, but that one must fear and adore him. According to Canon Drioton, who has collected an impressive number of these maxims, a true monotheism seems to occur which was superimposed on and even influenced traditional devotion.[10]

I am afraid that there is a great deal of fallacious interpretation in such a conclusion, however. The Egyptian language, especially that of ancient times, almost never employs the article, definite or indefinite. If, therefore, we find the word *ntjr* alone, we can envisage three translations: God, a god, or the god. We could only adopt the first if an Egyptian sage had plainly expressed the idea that there is only one God. This is not the case. The maxims of the sages, on the contrary, prove how far monotheism was from their thinking. Ptah-hotep says, "It is god *(ntjr)* who brings about progress."[11] Returning to the same idea Ani says, *"Your* god gives good luck."[12] In a similar sentence, Ani, having requested the celebration of his god's feast, explains that god will vent his anger against the one who neglects this duty.[13] In another passage Ani recommends silent prayer because god forbids loud noise in his dwelling.[14] This recommendation is directed to the inhabitant of Memphis who went to worship Ptah in his temple just as much as to the faithful worshiper of Osiris at Busiris and Abydos or to the faithful worshiper of Thoth at Khmunu. The use of *ntjr* without the possessive is therefore only a linguistic artifice which increases the scope of the maxims. I recognize too that this artifice is possible only because the majority of the

[10]Etienne Drioton, "La religion égyptienne," in *Histoire des religions*, ed. M. Brillant and R. Aigrain (Paris: Bloud et Gay, 1953———), III, 27.
[11]Ptah-hotep, verse 229.
[12]Ani, maxims 24-26.
[13]Ani, maxim 2.
[14]Ani, maxim 11.

great gods required the same virtues of their followers. Each one could, therefore, while remaining attached to the worship of his local god and without denying in the least the existence of other gods, use a language that is already monotheistic.

These remarks completely justify the way the Chronicler has the Pharaoh of Avaris speak in the above quoted passage. It would even be permissible to think that Moses, raised by an Egyptian princess as her son (Exod. 2:10) and very great in the eyes of Pharaoh's servants and the people of the land of Egypt (Exod. 11:3), knew and used the maxims which were in circulation in Egyptian conversation.

An idea that recurs repeatedly in the Bible is that the misfortunes of Israel and also individual misfortunes are the consequence of impiety. With some insignificant differences this idea is found in Egypt where the theme of disorder is periodically taken up by the scribes in terms that are almost identical. When the Old Kingdom fell apart after half a millennium, the regrets that this collapse inspired in a wise man of this period have come to us in a papyrus in the Leiden Museum, but many of its parts are missing:[15]

> "Alas, the Nile is overflowing, but no one works anymore because everyone says 'we do not know what will happen in this land' (pl. 2, 3).
> "Alas, the women are sterile; they no longer conceive; Khnum no longer builds because of the condition of the country (pl. 2, 4).
> "Alas, the dead are buried in the Nile; the water is a tomb; the water is a place of embalming (pl. 2, 6).
> "Alas, hearts are violent; the plague is prevalent throughout the land; blood is in every place; and

---

[15]Cf. text and translation in A. H. Gardiner, *The Admonitions of an Egyptian Sage* (Leipzig: J. C. Hinrichs, 1909).

Death is never idle (pl. 2, 5-6).
"Alas, the ship from the south is adrift; towns
are destroyed; Upper Egypt is a desert" (pl. 2, 11).

The priest Nefer-rohu, it is said, had foretold these
troubles as far back as the days of Snefru:

> "What had never yet happened is happening now. Arms
> are taken for warfare because the land lives in confu-
> sion . . . one man kills another. I will show you a son who
> has become an enemy, a brother who has become an op-
> ponent, a man who kills his father."[16]

In his turn, Ramses III recounts in broad strokes the
misfortunes of the past before summarizing his own reign:

> "The land of Egypt was adrift. Everyone had an enemy.
> For many years there had not been a leader until another
> age appeared when Egypt was under the more competent
> rule of sheiks. Each man murdered his brother."[17]

Could it not be said that Isaiah was acquainted with
these writings or others like them when he prophesied
what was going to happen to Egypt?

> "I will spur on Egypt against Egypt,
> And they shall fight, brother against brother and
>   neighbor against neighbor,
> City against city, and kingdom against kingdom. . . .
> . . . the river will be parched and dried up; . . .
> The Nile-arms of Egypt will dwindle and dry up;
> Reed and rush will wither, . . .
> . . . all that is sown by the Nile
> Will be dried up . . .
> The fishermen also will mourn and lament, . . .
> The workers in flax will be put to shame —
> The women who card and the men who weave
>   cotton— . . .
> All her workers for hire will be heartbroken"
>   (Isa. 19:2-10).

[16] Cf. the Ermitage (Leningrad) Papyrus 1116B in Pritchard, *op. cit.*,
pp. 444-46; A. H. Gardiner in *JEA*, I (1914), 100-106. The author of these
phrases, who lived during the XII dynasty, presents them as a prophecy.
[17] Cf. Papyrus Harris, I, 75, 3-4.

Public misfortunes were principally the result of the fact that Pharaoh had, because of the disobedience of his people, been placed in the impossible situation of having to fulfill his major obligation — the construction and endowment of temples. But everything returned to order when the gods had pity on Egypt and established a son of their flesh as king.[18]

The result of public or private impiety, namely the need to appeal to the gods, is clearly and forcefully expressed again at an earlier date:[19]

> What threatens the Egyptians if this holy place is deprived of its libations and offerings for the divine spirits that are there is as follows:
>
> The flood will be small at its source . . . there will be a year of famine in the whole land. There will be neither tree of life nor vegetables.
>
> If one does not act justly in his town in everything that concerns his temple, the insolence of enemies will be in the whole land.
>
> If one does not do all the ceremonies of Osiris in their time in this district and all the feasts on the calendar, this land will be deprived of its laws, the people will abandon their master and there will no longer be any regulations for the masses.
>
> If one does not do all the ceremonies of Osiris in their time, there will be a year of epidemic. The barbarians will carry away everything that exists in Egypt, people of the desert will revolt against Egypt, and there will be war and rebellion in all the land. The king in his palace will no longer be obeyed and the land will be deprived of defenders. Open the books, read the divine words and you will be wise, following the plans of the gods.

In these two lands equally exposed to natural catastrophe and to the encroachments of neighboring peoples, periods of prosperity were broken by periods of mourning,

[18]*Ibid.*, 75, 6-7.
[19]Jacques Vandier, *Le Papyrus Jumilhac* (Paris: Centre nationale de la recherche scientifique, 1961), XVII, 26—XVIII, 21.

anarchy, and invasion; and in each case it was lack of piety that had caused the evils and a return to piety that had healed them. This explanation of the facts could be presented spontaneously to the mind of observers in the two countries. Yet threats, exhortations, and lamentations are expressed in such a similar way that it may be concluded that wise men in both countries were familiar with writings from their own and neighboring lands in which misfortunes were foretold together with the appropriate remedies.[20]

THE DUTIES OF MAN ACCORDING TO THE ANCIENT SAGES

Egyptians hoped that the public, while visiting the tombs, would refrain from defacing the images and inscriptions and would fervently recite the formula, worth a good meal to them in Amenti (the Other World). To encourage them to carry out this pious rite, they did not forget to mention their value. Thus the stelae and inscriptions on walls allow us to draw up the following description of the honest man. He is a good son, a good subject of the king, a man of good company who never provokes quarrels but tries to stop them, a man who is also charitable because he gives bread to the hungry, water to those who are thirsty, clothing to the naked, and a trip across the Nile to those who have no boat. This, then, is the ideal man who will later inspire negative confessions.

Egyptians had minds too systematic not to have thought early of codifying the duties of man. The sage, Im-hotep, who lived at the time of Djoser, was undoubtedly the first

---

[20]H. O. Lange, *Prophezeiungen eines ägyptischen Weisen* (Berlin: A. Reimer, 1903); and Eduard Meyer, *Die Israeliten und ihre Nachbarstämme: Alttestamentliche Untersuchungen* (Halle: M. Niemeyer, 1906). Both have maintained that the prophetic books of the Egyptians were the principle source of Hebrew prophetism. Such a radical opinion now appears to have been abandoned.

author of instructions;[21] he was followed by many others. Passing over those instructions which exist only in fragmentary form, we shall refer first to those that were composed during the reign of Snefru for Ka'gemni, of which we have only the ending (see Posener's article, p. 31, No. 2); then to the Maxims of Ptah-hotep during the reign of Izozi, known through several manuscripts (p. 32, No. 4). The First Intermediate Period has left us instructions composed for Pharaoh Meri-ka-Re by his father, Pharaoh Wah-ka-Re Khety II (p. 34, No. 10); and the Middle Kingdom, those of Amen-em-het I (p. 37, No. 23), of an unknown man to his son (p. 37, No. 26), of Khety the son of Duauf known as the Satire on the Trades (p. 36, No. 23), of Sehetep-ib-Re (Amen-em-het I) to his children (p. 37, No. 27 A). From the New Kingdom, we have the almost complete educational instructions of the scribe Ani (p. 42, No. 53) and other educational instructions from a sage named Ameni (p. 42, No. 55), which is perhaps the re-editing of an older writing. The period following the New Kingdom has left us a work which has become famous since its publication: "the teaching of life, the testimony for prosperity," composed by a land survey and grain scribe, Amen-em-Opet (p. 43, No. 58).[22] This person spent part of his life (at a time we cannot pinpoint; probably under the XXII dynasty) meditating in the capital of the Great Land nome, and possessed a cenotaph in Abydos. It is at Senut, however, in the Min nome that

[21]An inventory of Egyptian literary works, didactic works, novels, and tales, has been drawn up by Georges Posener, "Les richesses inconnues de la littérature égyptienne," *Revue d'égyptologie*, VI (1951), 27-48. Imhotep's instruction appears as Number 1 on p. 31.

[22]Cf. the British Museum Papyrus 10474, published in facsimile by Sir E. A. T. Wallis Budge, *Facsimiles of Egyptian Hieratic Papyri in the British Museum. Second Series* (London: British Museum, 1923), pls. I–XIV; and his *The Teaching of Amen-em-âpt, Son of Ka-nakht* (London: M. Hopkinson and Co., 1924), as well as the hieroglyphic transcription of H. O. Lange, *Das Weisheitsbuch des Amenemope. Aus dem Papyrus 10474 des British Museum* (Copenhagen: K. Dansk Videnskabernes Selskab, 1925).

his tomb is located. He married a singer belonging to the temple of Shu and Tefnut, divinities of This, and had a son by her, Hor the Triumphant, priest of Min, to whom the work is dedicated.[23]

In this long series of works we will omit those that are attributed to pharaohs, or those that have loyalty to the sovereign as their object so we can consider those of more universal significance.

Rather than a moral treatise, the teaching of Ptah-hotep is a handbook on how to live in which the reader learns how to get along with his wife, with the wives of others, and with his superiors; and what to do when one is a guest or involved in a quarrel. This wisdom is somewhat prosaic, as Adolf Erman has so well said.[24] He, on the contrary, holds the educational instructions of the scribe Ani to be among the most delightful works in all Egyptian literature.[25] Many maxims would justify this judgment but none more than that which exorts the reader to venerate and love his mother:

> Give her bread in abundance and carry her as she has carried you. You were a heavy load for her; when you were born after your months she still carried you on her shoulders and for three years her breast was in your mouth . . . she sent you to school . . . and every day she waited there with bread and beer from her own home.[26]

This passage and many others that we could extract from the wisdom literature of Egyptians would not detract from that of the Hebrews. But when Moses says to the sons of Israel: "You must not imitate the practices of the land of Egypt in which you lived" (Lev. 18:3), he is obviously prejudiced and even ungrateful.

---

[23]The only information we have on Amen-em-Opet is that contained in the papyrus a judge as competent as A. H. Gardiner is satisfied to place anywhere between the XXI and the XXVI dynasties.

[24]Adolf Erman, *op. cit.*, p. 192.

[25]*Ibid.*, pp. 192-93.

[26]Cf. Pritchard, *ANET*, p. 420.

THE INSTRUCTION OF AMEN-EM-OPET
AND THE BOOK OF PROVERBS

At an earlier date the parallelism between the wisdom of the Hebrews and that of Egypt is still more evident. The first editor and all the translators of the Instruction of Amen-em-Opet[27] have emphasized the resemblances which allow them to compare a number of Egyptian maxims with passages from the book of Proverbs, especially in its third section (22:17 — 24:22). Sometimes it could almost be said that one of the texts is a translation of the other. But this resemblance can be explained in many ways. Egyptologists have readily admitted for the most part that the work of Amen-em-Opet was the direct source of this third section and their opinion has convinced other scholars. An Egyptologist, Canon Drioton, has recently reversed the order, however, and maintained that Amen-em-Opet has plagiarized an ancient work of Israelite wisdom, extracts of which are found in the book of Proverbs.[28]

Chronology does not enable us to solve the problem. The Bible itself attributes the last section of Proverbs to Hezekiah (Prov. 25:1), but this information has not been particularly helpful for the earlier sections. As for Amen-

---

[27]Cf. Pritchard, *ANET*, pp. 421-25. There are two complete translations of the Instruction of Amen-em-Opet, one by Lange (No. 31), the other by F. Llewellyn Griffith, "The Teaching of Amenophis, the Son of Kanakht. Papyrus B. M. 10474," *JEA*, XII (1926), 191-237; both are very able works. Difficulties remain, because the author frequently uses rare or poetic words and baffling expressions. In his commentary, Griffith does not fail to point out corresponding passages from the Bible. On these parallels cf. again Adolf Erman, *Eine ägyptische Quelle der "Sprüche Salomos"* (Berlin: Sitzungsberichte, 1924); D. C. Simpson, "The Hebrew Book of Proverbs and the Teaching of Amenophis," *JEA*, XII (1926), 232-39; B. Gemser, *Sprüche Salomos* (Tübingen: J. C. B. Mohr [Paul Siebeck], 1937), p. 65; *Le Livre des Proverbes* (2 vols.; Paris: Desclée de Brouwer, 1938), pp. 465-68, Vol. I in Hilaire Duesberg, *Les scribes inspirés: Introduction aux Livres sapientiaux de la Bible;* Hilaire Duesberg and P. Auvray, *Le Livre des Proverbes* (Paris: Editions du Cerf, 1951), p. 20.

[28]Etienne Drioton, "Sur la Sagesse d'Amonemope," in *Mélanges bibliques André Robert* (Paris: Bloud et Gay, 1957), pp. 254-80. Pritchard also refers to R. O. Kevin, *The Wisdom of Amen-em-apt and Its Possible Dependence Upon the Hebrew Book of Proverbs* (Philadelphia, 1931).

em-Opet, all we know about him is what he says in his preface. He fails to name the pharaoh who conferred his functions on him. Neither language nor paleography permits us to pinpoint its date. As able a judge as Sir Alan H. Gardiner lets Amen-em-Opet drift between the beginning of the XXI dynasty and the Saïtic age.[29]

Canon Drioton has proposed to show that Amen-em-Opet spoke an Egyptian form of Hebrew. It is not impossible to discover a number of Hebraisms in his work, but they are not as numerous as has been suggested.[30] The cultured class could, in an age when so many Jews were seeking refuge in the Delta and even in Upper Egypt, borrow certain expressions from the language of their visitors. But it seems to me that the subject matter is more significant than the form in this case and that one cannot read the Instruction of Amen-em-Opet without being struck by its authentically Egyptian character, a character that it could not possess to the same degree if its author had borrowed from a foreign work. It is, on the contrary, the author of Proverbs who, in spite of the care which he has taken to cut out the numerous allusions to Egyptian things that abound in his model, acknowledges his dependence in the first verses of the third section: "Have I not written for you these thirty sayings respecting counsel and knowledge that you may bring back a true report to him who sends you?" (Prov. 22:20-21).

The Instruction of Amen-em-Opet is also divided into thirty *ḥwt* (chapters).[31] But while this division in the work of the Hebrew sage does not have any plausible ex-

[29]A. H. Gardiner, "Writing and Literature," in S. R. K. Glanville, *The Legacy of Egypt* (Oxford: Clarendon Press, 1942), pp. 67-70.

[30]The expression "way of life" which appears in the title of the educational instructions of Ameni cannot be considered as a Hebraism; cf. Posener, *op. cit.*, No. 55. Nor can the expression "incline your ears" that one finds in the Semnieh and Paheri stelae; cf. *UAA*, IV, 496, 114.

[31]The word is already attested in the texts of the pyramids; cf. *WAS*, ed. A. Erman and H. Grapow, III, 6.

planation, it did have a meaning for the Egyptian author
who mentions (p. XX, 1, 18) the advice of the Thirty, a
sort of high court of justice. Just as the faithful worshiper,
while pronouncing the negative confession, denies suc-
cessively having committed forty-two sins because there
are forty-two nomes whose representatives surround Osiris,
Amen-em-Opet dedicates to each of the thirty judges one
of the chapters of his work.

Moreover his preface conforms completely to the rules
established by the ancient sages of Egypt:

> The beginning of the teaching of life
> The testimony for prosperity
> All the rules for . . .
> The customs for courtiers
> To know how to answer the question asked, to send a
> report to
> The one who sent it,
> To direct yourself on the way of life . . .
> Composed by the officer in charge of the land (his
> other titles follow)
> Amen-em-Opet, the son of Ka-nakht . . .
> For his son, the youngest of his children,
> Hor-em-maa-kheru . . .

It is to this son that the first verses of the first chapter
are specifically addressed:

> Give your ears, listen to what is said,
> Give your heart to understand it.
> It is worthwhile to hide them in your heart,
> Misfortune to the one who rejects them . . .
> If you spend your time with them in your heart
> You will find that it is a good thing indeed.

It was continuous tradition in ancient Egypt for every
author of maxims, king and private individual alike, to
address himself to his son, real or supposed. The aged
Ptah-hotep molded his son to be a support to his old age
and proposed to teach him that eloquence which would

delight the one who heard it and bring misfortune to the one who paid no attention to it.[32]

Influenced by this Egyptian tradition, the author of Proverbs reveals to us at the beginning the name of the author — Solomon, the son of David — and the purpose of the book — to give discernment to the simple, knowledge and reflection to the young man. "Listen, my son, to your father's instruction," Solomon continues. These words "my son" occur at the beginning of several chapters, but the beginning of the third chapter is quite clearly an imitation of the exhortation of Amen-em-Opet:

> Incline your ear, and hear the words of the wise
> And apply your mind to know them
> For it is well that you should keep them within
> you . . . (Prov. 22:17-18) .

The advantages of wisdom and the consequences of bad behavior are, moreover, expressed throughout the book of Proverbs. Having thus won the attention of their readers in the same way, the two moralists, the Egyptian and the Hebrew, are in agreement on general principles and on the majority of their applications. The basic principle is that we are not masters of our destiny. Ptah-hotep had earlier written, "It is not the plan of men which becomes a reality; it is the will of God."[33]

In his turn, Amen-em-Opet will say:

> Success is in the hand of the god (Amen-em-Opet, XIV, 1)
> God is always in your success
> and man in your failure.
> One thing the words that men say,
> another thing what the god does (Amen-em-Opet, XIX, 14-17) .

---

[32]The Instruction of the Vizier Ptah-hotep, verses 48-50; cf. Pritchard, *ANET*, p. 412.
[33]*Ibid.*, verses 115-16.

This antithesis is familiar to the author of Proverbs: "Commit your business to the Lord and your plans will prosper" (Prov. 16:3).

The dignity of the poor and the sick must never be lost from view. Amen-em-Opet never tires of repeating it:

> Poverty in the hand of the god is better
> Than riches in a storehouse (Amen-em-Opet, IX, 5-6).
> Praise as one who loves men is better
> Than riches in a storehouse;
> Bread when the heart is overflowing is better
> Than riches with worries (Amen-em-Opet, XVI, 11-14).

This thought will inspire La Fontaine's fable of the Cobbler and the Financier, but the emphasis becomes even more marked in the following chapter:

> Do not make fun of a blind man nor be insulting to
> a dwarf . . .
> Do not rail at a man who is the hand of god [i.e., the
> insane]
> Do not turn your back on him if he errs.
> For man is clay and straw
> And god is his architect (Amen-em-Opet, XXIV, 9-14).

Here we recognize the man of the Nile Valley, where baked brick made of lime and straw was the usual building material. The author of Proverbs has not retained this figure of speech but he too holds poverty in high esteem:

> A good name is more desirable than great riches
> A good reputation than silver and gold.
> The rich and the poor meet face to face
> The Lord is the maker of them both (Prov. 22:1-2).
> Better a little, with righteousness
> Than great revenues with injustice (Prov. 16:8).
> Better a morsel of dry bread, and peace with it,
> Than a house full of feasting, with discord (Prov. 17:1).

This thought is to control the attitude, especially of the judge and the scribe, to the poor:

> The one who respects the poor is loved by God
> More than the one who honors the rich (Amen-em-Opet, XXVI, 3-4).
> Do not desire the property of the poor man,
> Do not hunger for his bread.
> The property of the poor man is a plug in the throat
> It causes nausea in the gullet (Amen-em-Opet, XIV, 5-8).

The author of Proverbs has kept this image but he applies it to different circumstances:

> Dine not with a miserly man
> And lust not after his dainties;
> For they will be like storm in the throat and nausea in the gullet . . .
> You must spit out the morsel you have eaten . . .
>   (Prov. 23:6-8).

This disagreeable result awaits the one who reluctantly accepts the invitation of someone richer than himself.

The following commandment seems to come directly from an Egyptian source:

> Rob not the poor because he is poor
> And crush not the needy in the gate (Prov. 22:22).

The moralists of the Middle Kingdom already object strongly to the harshness with which judges treated the poor.[34] The reference to "in the gate," which has puzzled exegetes, is quite naturally explained by the well attested Egyptian custom of rendering justice at the temple gates.[35]

The rapidity with which property wrongly acquired disappeared struck both moralists. The Egyptian author says:

---

[34]P. Montet, *VQ*, pp. 250-51.
[35]Serge Sauneron "La justice à la porte des temples," *Bulletin de l'Institut français d'archéologie orientale du Caire*, LIV (1954), 117.

> If you acquire property by theft
> It will not spend the night with you.
> In the morning it will no longer be in your house;
> You will see its place but it will not be there . . .
> It will have made itself wings like geese
> and have flown to the heavens . . . (Amen-em-Opet, IX,
>   16; X, 4).

The Hebrew author says:

> Toil not to become rich;
> Seek not superfluous wealth!
> Scarcely have you set your eye upon it when it is gone;
> For riches make themselves wings
> Like an eagle that flies toward the heavens
>   (Prov. 23:4-5).

The similarity is obvious, except that riches which so quickly and easily change hands suggest the flight of geese to the Egyptian, and the flight of an eagle to the Hebrew. The eagle is almost unknown in ancient Egypt. The flight of the falcon is mentioned concerning pharaoh or gods who abandon the earth for heaven. The geese Amen-em-Opet thinks of are not those raised on farms, but the migrating geese that gather periodically in the region of the Upper Nile.[36] As he has done in other passages, the Hebrew adapter suppresses or modifies a specifically Egyptian detail.

The respect of parents is a universal obligation. Amen-em-Opet, writing for his son, did not think it necessary to insist on this; but the author of Proverbs orders:

> Listen to the father who begot you,
> And despise not your mother when she is old
>   (Prov. 23:22).

It would not be difficult to find analogous expressions

[36]G. Lefebvre, *RCE*, p. 219.

121

in Egyptian literature; we have already quoted the touching words that gratitude inspired in the scribe Ani.[37]

Amen-em-Opet says nothing about the punishment of children, whereas according to Proverbs 23:13 it is necessary:

> Withhold not chastisement from a child.
> For if you beat him with the rod, he will not die.

The stick played such a significant role in ancient Egypt we cannot imagine that it was not used on children now and then. A child's ear is on his back, says an ill-tempered scribe.[38] In the story of Cheops and the magicians, a maid-servant is corrected by her brother.[39] Within reasonable limits a husband could beat his wife.[40] Parents were very lenient with their children, but that does not mean the father did not sometimes use the whip.[41]

Among the ideas familiar to the ancient wise men as far back as the days of Ptah-hotep is the following:

> Contact with wicked men should be avoided
> And answering when provoked should be shunned.[42]

The same idea is expressed in the Instruction of Amen-em-Opet and in Proverbs:

> Do not sit down with an irritable man
> Do not seek his conversation (Amen-em-Opet, XI, 13-14).
> Form no friendship with a hot-tempered man
> And with a passionate man go not

---

[37]*Supra*, p. 114.

[38]Ricardo A. Caminos, *Late Egyptian Miscellanies* (London: Oxford University Press, 1954), p. 83.

[39]Lefebvre, *op. cit.*, p. 90.

[40]P. Montet, *VQ*, p. 59.

[41]Examples of such leniency are given in the story of Setna; cf. Gaston Maspéro, *CP*, p. 106. A similar example is given in the story of the Prince Elect; cf. Lefebvre, *RCE*, pp. 119-22.

[42]Cf. A. Erman, *op. cit.*, p. 193.

Lest you learn his ways . . . (Prov. 22:24-25).
Do not say, "Find me a defender
For one who hates me has injured me,"
Because you do not know the plans of god
and you cannot understand the morrow.
Rest in the hands of god
Until your silence has triumphed over him (Amen-em-
   Opet, XXII, 3-8).
Do not say "I will pay back evil!"
Wait for the Lord to help you (Prov. 20:22).

All Egyptian moralists advocate the practice of temperance and the avoidance of drunkards. Although grapevines were cultivated in the Delta and their products transported to Assuan, the national drink was beer, and it was chiefly beer that inveterate drinkers drank to excess.[43] Amen-em-Opet says nothing about this matter but Proverbs condemned both intemperance (23:20) and intoxication (23: 30-32).

Lying is one of the sins forbidden in the negative confession.[44] In many of the Middle Kingdom stelae the following sentence occurs: "Lying is an abomination to me."[45] Amen-em-Opet adds his voice to its condemnation:

Do not falsely pretend to give a man secret information;
That is an abomination to god (Amen-em-Opet, XIII,
   15-16).
God hates a man who speaks falsely;
His great abomination is duplicity (Amen-em-Opet,
   XIV, 2).

This thought is found in Proverbs:

Lying lips are an abomination to the Lord,
But those who deal truthfully are his delight
   (Prov. 12:22).

---

[43]Herodotus, II, 59-60, does say, however, that more wine was drunk at Bubastis during the feasts than in all of Egypt during the rest of the year.
[44]Version B, sentences 9 and 24.
[45]Hapi-Djefai at Assiut; cf. Pierre Montet, "Les Tombeaux de Siout et de Deir Rifeh," *Kêmi,* IV (1935), 53.

Too much speaking is harmful. Amen-em-Opet describes himself as *Grw maʻa* (silent and truthful).[46] It was a duty in certain nomes not to reveal what one knew of holy things.[47]

This maxim gives an example:

> Do not spread your words to the common people
> Nor associate with a man who babbles (Amen-em-Opet, XXII, 13-14).

Similarly in Proverbs:

> A talebearer reveals secrets
> So have nothing to do with a gossip (Prov. 20:19)

And again:

> The man who conceals what he knows is better
> Than the one who expresses it injuriously (Amen-em-Opet, XXII, 15-16).

The same idea occurs as follows in Proverbs:

> A man of sense conceals what he knows;
> But fools proclaim their folly (Prov. 12:23).

Honesty in business and administrative matters was only an application of these principles. Egyptians were very attached to them. In his confession a deceased man twice declares that he had not falsified weights and once declares that he has not cut down the size of a bushel. Amen-em-Opet, who during his lifetime was in charge of lands and seeding, tax assessment on grains, measurement of islands and new lands constantly modified by the retreat of the Nile between two flood periods, and the establishment of landmarks on field boundaries, was not supposed to joke

[46]An individual whose statue was found at Tanis is also thus described; cf. P. Montet, "Inscriptions de Basse Époque trouvées à Tanis," *Kêmi*, XV (1959), pp. 50-51.

[47]P. Montet, "Le Fruit défendu," *Kêmi*, XI (1951), 106.

about these matters. Here are his recommendations concerning weight:

> The baboon stands near the balance
> And his heart is its spring
> What god is like Thoth the great
> Who found these things in order to use them?
> Do not use false weights in your work (Amen-em-Opet,
> XVII, 22; XVIII, 1-4).

The support of the scales is frequently surmounted either by a baboon, the image of the god Thoth, or by Ma'et, goddess of truth (fig. 19).[48]

Figure 19. WEIGHING GOLD

Chapter eighteen of Amen-em-Opet is almost completely dedicated to the measurement of grain (fig. 20).[49]

> Take care not to alter the *wedjat*
> Nor to falsify its fractions (Amen-em-Opet, XVIII, 15-16).
> Do not make two different bushel measures,
> For that must be done only for flood waters.
> The bushel is Re's eye.
> The one who cheats is an abomination to him.
> As for the measurer who repeatedly steals
> His eye confirms the accusation against him
>   (Amen-em-Opet, XVIII, 19; XIX, 3).

[48]The Theben Tombs Series, Vol. III, pl. IX.
[49]*Ibid.*, pl. X.

Figure 20. Grain Measured by the Bushel

The *wedjat*, a unit of grain measurement, was none other than Horus' eye, broken into fragments by Seth and restored by Thoth. Its pieces had values of decreasing worth.[50]

To change landmarks certainly constituted a grave offense in ancient Egypt, the more so because flooding

[50]Griffith, *art. cit.*, p. 228; A. H. Gardiner, *EG*, p. 197.

Figure 21. Surveyors at Work

126

washed them out or shifted them when the water receded and people had difficulty identifying their own property. This gave rise to a need for a group of surveyors (fig. 21), and to these warnings of Amen-em-Opet:

> Do not remove landmarks from the edges of fields,
> Nor change the position of measuring lines
> Do not covet a single cubit of land
> Nor encroach upon a widow's land (Amen-em-Opet, VII, 12-16).

As for the land defrauder:

> His house is an enemy of the town
> His granaries are destroyed.
> His property is seized by his children's hands,
> And his possessions are given to another (Amen-em-Opet, VIII, 4-8).

This strictness concerning weight, volume, and length measurements to which Egyptians attached so much value also occurs in Proverbs, where it is almost impossible to question an Egyptian background:

> Diverse weights, diverse measures—
> Both of them alike are an abomination to the Lord (Prov. 20:10).
> Balance and scales are set by the Lord;
> All the weights in the bag are his concern. (Prov. 16:11).
> Diverse weights are an abomination to the Lord
> And false scales are not good (Prov. 20:23).

As might be expected, Proverbs does not speak of Thoth and his baboon, nor of Ma'et, nor of Amon and his ram with the measuring tape twisted around its neck; but boundaries are also something that must not be touched:

Remove not the ancient landmark
Which your fathers set up (Prov. 22:28).
Remove not the widow's landmark
Nor enter the fields of orphans
For their champion is strong
And he will defend their cause against you
   (Prov. 23:10-11).

Fraud was even more serious if the victim was a widow
or orphan. The two moralists agree on that point, but it
should not be forgotten that ancient treaties, stelae, and
negative confessions also prohibit any wish to oppress
them.

To bring this résumé of maxims belonging to both
sages to a close, here is a passage in which Amen-em-Opet
sets forth the proper way for the pious Egyptian to behave
in the temple:

As for the heated man in the temple
He is like a tree planted in the forest
That in a moment loses its leaves
And ends up in the shipyards . . .
The man who is silent and tells the truth stands
   apart.
He is like a tree planted in an orchard
That becomes green and produces its fruit.
It is in its master's presence (Amen-em-Opet, VI, 1-8).

If it is true that worship in Egypt was the business of
the priesthood, that does not mean that the masses were
in any way kept out of the temple. A wish is made that a
woman may drink sweet wine or ordinary wine as she
likes in the outer court of the Temple of Neith.[51] People
went with the god on his travels, and Herodotus[52] and
Juvenal[53] mention people who put so much energy into

[51]Inscription on a vase from Bubastis; cf. Pierre Montet. *Les reliques
de l'art syrien* (Paris: Les Belles Lettres, 1937), p. 142.
[52]Herodotus, II, 63.
[53]Juvenal, Satire 15 at the beginning.

acting out ventures of the gods that men were injured and even killed in the process. The sage thinks of them when he contrasts the heated man in front of the temple with the man who is silent and tells the truth and who stands apart.

The author of Proverbs has not seen fit to include this passage, but Jeremiah, on the other hand, seems to have remembered it when he compares the man who trusts in man with the man who trusts in God. The first:

> ". . . shall be like a shrub in the desert,
> Unable to see the coming of good.
> He shall dwell in the scorched lands of the wilderness,
> In an uninhabited salt land" (Jer. 17:6).

But the second:

> ". . . shall be like a tree planted by waters
> That sends out its roots to the stream;
> And is not afraid when heat comes,
> For its leaves remain green;
> Nor is anxious in a year of drought,
> For it ceases not to bear fruit" (Jer. 17:8).

Unless I am mistaken, the foregoing quotations prove that Amen-em-Opet was not a unique individual in his homeland. Rather, as heir of a long tradition of wise men who since the time of the Old Kingdom had done their best to establish the principles, applications, and advantages of eloquence, he taught nothing new. He was content to express advice that had been given before and that he did not need to ask foreigners to keep, and he did so in his own way and in an affected style that is often obscure for us and was perhaps crammed with foreign expressions. An Egyptian speaking to all Egyptians and not just to those of the nomes where he lived out his life, he made many allusions to the gods of Egypt,[54] as well as to matters

---

[54]Cf. those at the end of Griffith, *art. cit.*, pp. 227-31.

pertaining to the Nile Valley, the sometimes unpleasant north wind, crocodiles, and institutions such as the Council of the Thirty.

The similarities between the Instruction of Amen-em-Opet and the book of Proverbs are too close and too numerous to be the result of chance. They have helped the first interpreters of Amen-em-Opet and even recent interpreters of Proverbs greatly. Since we have rejected the idea that Amen-em-Opet used Proverbs or some ancient work of Israelite wisdom whose existence has not been proved, we must align ourselves with those first translators of Amen-em-Opet who found the direct source of a whole section of Proverbs in his instruction.

With B. Gemser,[55] we readily admit that the Hebrew moralist has not composed a slavish imitation of the Instruction of Amen-em-Opet. He has willingly omitted the Egyptian setting, the gods of the Nile Valley, the crocodiles and the north wind. However, he has retained references to the thirty chapters of the Instruction and allusions to the disputes that took place in the gates which also appear to be of Egyptian origin. He has not retained the order (or disorder, if you prefer) of his model, but although he has given his maxims a typically Hebrew flavor he has not attempted to hide what he owes to Amen-em-Opet and to the whole host of Egyptian moralists of which Amen-em-Opet was a part.

THE WISDOM OF PETOSIRIS

It would, however, be highly unlikely that Israel's prophets and wise men did not in their turn influence the Egyptian elite, especially from the time of the Jewish flight from Assyrian or Babylonian invasion and their consequent spread to the towns of the eastern Delta, On, Memphis, and Upper Egypt.

[55]Gemser, *op. cit.*, p. 69.

Traces of this influence are above all evident in the inscriptions of the priest of Thoth who lived at Khmunu at the beginning of the Ptolemaic era. G. Lefebvre, who published these inscriptions, has emphasized the parallels between some of the maxims of Petosiris and certain verses in the Bible. The following quotations, borrowed from his work, show the sage seeking God in the darkness and finding happiness by walking in his ways:

> I have yearned for thee in the night,
> With all my heart I seek thee (Isa. 26:9).
> All night long god's spirit was in my soul
> From dawn have I done what He desired (Petosiris, 116).
> How happy is everyone who fears the Lord,
> Who walks in his ways! (Ps. 128:1).
> The path of the one who is faithful to god is (good).
> Blessed is the one whose heart directs him to it (Petosiris, 116).

The priest of Thoth also developed his conception of happiness in inscriptions 60 and 61. Yet, as Lefebvre has very correctly noted, the Hebrew and the Egyptian did not draw the same conclusion from their premises. As a reward for his obedience the Hebrew expected only an earthly reward, a long and happy life in the midst of his children's children. But the Egyptian saw beyond death an eternal reward with the gods he had served during his lifetime.

CONCLUSION

Conclusion

Scholars have long wondered if the descent of Israel into the land of the pharaohs, the settling in the Land of Goshen, the Oppression, and the Exodus were not just so many stories without historical foundation. Having thought that the problem was resolved, we have attempted to prove their authenticity as we have gone along. The Abraham episode fits as naturally as can be into the XII dynasty. The story of Joseph and his brothers takes place when the royal court is at Avaris — during the rule of the Hyksos kings, to be exact. About four centuries later Ramses II built a palace on the ruins of Avaris where he and his successors would spend the greater part of the year. As much to recruit manpower as to guarantee the security of the royal court, he was led to modify his policy with respect to Israel. The Israelites were content just to groan as long as Ramses lived, but the difficulties that beset Mer-ne-Ptah toward the middle of his reign gave them the chance to leave Egypt in order to take possession of the land that Yahweh had given them as an inheritance. These great events are admirably summed up in these words from Deuteronomy: "A nomad Aramean was my father; he went down to Egypt to reside there, with a small company, and there he became a nation, great, mighty and numerous" (26:5).

It is very remarkable that at three crucial moments the sons of Israel found the pharaoh and his court at the same place, a place first called Avaris, then Ramses, and finally Tanis.

When the Chronicler undertook to give Israel's memories of the past a definitive form, those memories had not been forgotten. If a few insignificant anachronisms were introduced into the Joseph story, they do not take away much from the credibility of a narrative in which nothing occurs that would shock the Egyptologist accustomed to the tales and stories that circulated in the Nile Valley, and to the pictures that its painters have given us of Egyptian life.

Very desirous not to imitate their oppressors and even on certain important points to go counter to what they did, the sons of Israel could not shut their eyes to the piety and moral qualities of the Egyptian people. The Ten Commandments are basically a negative confession, and the Bible recognizes this fact by stating that Moses was versed in the wisdom of the Egyptians.

The creation of the Kingdom of Judah did not put an end to intercourse between the Hebrews and the Egyptians. For centuries nomads had crossed the borders when they were harried by famine or terrorized by an implacable foe. The Hebrew people continued to look in the direction of Egypt to escape massacre or deportation. We now have a remarkable witness to the influence which this contact with Egypt exerted — the Instruction of Amen-em-Opet which, purged of everything that had an exclusively Egyptian character, finally became the Proverbs of Solomon.

CHRONOLOGICAL CHART, BIBLIOGRAPHY, INDEXES

Chronological Chart

DATE B.C.	EGYPTIAN HISTORY	BIBLICAL HISTORY

2000 ⎧
⸺ ⎨
1800 ⎩
	XII Dynasty
	Court at It-Tawy
	Exploitation of Turquoise
	   Mines
	Relations with Byblos, Ugarit,
	   Qatna
		Abraham's Descent
		into Egypt

1800 ⸺	Decline and Division of Egypt God Seth All-powerful at Avaris	
1675	The Hyksos Occupy Egypt to Cusae Avaris Their Capital	Joseph Sold to Egypt Joseph's Promotion The Sons of Israel Settle in Goshen
ca. 1600	Ka-mose, Prince of Thebes, Undertakes Liberation of Egypt	
1580	Recapture of Avaris Foundation of XVIII Dynasty Wars and Conquests in Syria	Death of Joseph Sons of Israel in Goshen
1321 ⎫ 1314 ⎭	XIX Dynasty Founded; The Era of Menophres	
1301	Ramses II; Per-Ramses Built as Royal Residence; Construction of Pithom and Red Sea Canal in the East- ern Delta	The Sons of Israel Are Regimented and Forced to Work at Per-Ram- ses and Pithom

139

DATE B.C.	EGYPTIAN HISTORY	BIBLICAL HISTORY
1235	Mer-ne-Ptah	Birth of Moses Moses and Aaron Speak before Pharaoh
1230	Libyan Invasion	The Exodus
1195	Ramses III	
ca. 1100	Social Problems Civil War Destruction of Per-Ramses and Avaris Suppression of the Seth Cult	Conquest of Palestine
1085	Smendes at Tanis Wen-amon's Trip to Byblos	
1054	Psusennes Improves Tanis and Marries a Chaldean Princess	Saul David David's Enemy, Hadad, Welcomed to Egypt and His Return to Edom after David's Death
	Siamon Seizes Gezer	Solomon Marries Pharaoh's Daughter Who Brings Gezer as a Dowry
	Increasing Importance of Maa Leaders	Jeroboam Welcomed in Egypt
950	Sheshonk I Palestine Campaign Contacts with Byblos	Capture of Jerusalem in the Fifth Year of Rehoboam
929	Osorkon I Contacts with Byblos	
ca. 890		Asa Stops an Ethiopian Invasion

Chronological chart

DATE B.C.	EGYPTIAN HISTORY	BIBLICAL HISTORY
870	Osorkon II Improves Tanis	
1080 } 680	Amen-em-Opet Composes an Instruction	
727–722		Shalmaneser V
716	Bocchoris (Bak-en-renef)	Coming of Ezekiel
705		Death of Sargon
689	Tirhakah	Sennacherib Fights Tirhakah
671		Esarhaddon Seizes Memphis
667	Sack of Thebes	
663	Psamtik (Psammetichus) Founds XXVI Dynasty	
640		Josiah
609	Necho Restores the Red Sea Canal Necho Victorious at Megiddo	Josiah Killed by Necho at Megiddo, Replaced by Jehoiakim
605	Necho Defeated at Carchemish	
588	Apries (Hophra)	Fall of Jerusalem Jeremiah Taken to Egypt
581		End of the Kingdom of Judah

Bibliography

Cambridge Ancient History. Rev. ed. of Vols. I and II. Cambridge: University Press, 1961——

Černý, Jaroslav. *Ancient Egyptian Religion.* London and New York: Hutchinson's University Library, 1957.

Dhorme, Edouard. *L'Ancien Testament,* Vol. I of *La Bible.* Bibliothèque NRF de la Pleiade; Paris: Gallimard, 1956.

Drioton, Etienne, and Jacques Vandier. *L'Egypte,* Vol. II of *Les peuples de l'Orient mediterranéen.* ("Collection Clio.") 4th ed.; Paris: Presses Universitaires de France, 1962.

Duesberg, Dom Hilaire, and P. Auvray. *Le Livre des Proverbes.* Paris: Editions du Cerf, 1951.

Erman, Adolf. *Ägypten und ägyptisches Leben in Altertum.* Revised by Hermann Ranke. Tübingen: J. C. B. Mohr (Paul Siebeck), 1923. (Eng. trans. of 1st ed.: *Life in Ancient Egypt,* trans. H. M. Tirard [London and New York: Macmillan and Co., 1894].)

————. *A Handbook of Egyptian Religion.* New York: E. P. Dutton and Co., 1907.

————. *The Literature of the Ancient Egyptians.* Translated by A. M. Blackman. London: Methuen and Co., Ltd., 1927.

————. *La religion des Egyptiens.* Translated by Henri Wild. Paris: Payot, 1937.

Erman, Adolf, and Hermann Grapow (eds.). *Wörterbuch der ägyptischen Sprache.* 7 vols. Leipzig: J. C. Hinrichs, 1926-1963.

Gardiner, A. H. "The Delta Residence of the Ramessides," *Journal of Egyptian Archaeology,* V (1918), 127, 179, 242.

————. "The Ancient Military Road Between Egypt and Palestine," *Journal of Egyptian Archaeology*, VI (1920), 90.

————. *Egyptian Grammar* (2nd ed.; London: G. Cumberlege, 1950).

————. "The Geography of the Exodus," *Journal of Egyptian Archaeology*, X (1924), 93.

————. "The Egyptian Origin of Some English Personal Names," *Journal of the American Oriental Society*, LVI (1936), 192-94.

Gauthier, Henri. *Dictionnaire des noms géographiques contenus dans les textes hiéroglyphiques.* 7 vols. Cairo: Imprimerie de l'Institut français d'archéologie orientale, 1925-1931.

————. *Le Livre des Rois d'Egypte.* 5 vols. in 6. Cairo: Imprimerie de l'Institut français d'archéologie orientale, 1907-1917.

Gemser, B. *Sprüche Salomos.* Vol. XVI in Otto Eissfeldt (ed.), *Handbuch zum Alten Testament.* Tübingen: J. C. B. Mohr (Paul Siebeck), 1937.

Griffith, F. Llewellyn. "The Teaching of Amenophis, the Son of Ka-nakht. Papyrus B. M. 10474," *Journal of Egyptian Archaeology*, XII (1926), 191-231.

Kitchen, K. A. *The Joseph Narrative and Its Egyptian Background.* Liverpool: Liverpool University Press, 1962.

Lange, H. O. *Das Weisheitsbuch des Amenemope. Aus dem Papyrus 10474 des British Museum.* Copenhagen: K. Dansk Videnskabernes Selshab, 1925.

Lefebvre, Gustave (ed. and trans.). *Romans et contes égyptiens de l'époque pharaoniques.* Paris: A. Maisonneuve, 1949.

Lods, Adolfe. *Israël, des origines au milieu du VIIIe siècle.* Paris: La Renaissance du Livre, 1935. (Eng. trans.: *Israel From Its Beginnings to the Middle of the Eighth Century*, trans. S. H. Hooke [London: Kegan Paul, Trench, Trübner and Co., Ltd., 1932].)

————. *Les prophètes d'Israël et les débuts du judaïsme.* Paris: La Renaissance du Livre, 1935. (Eng. trans.: *The Prophets and the Rise of Judaism*, trans. S. H. Hooke [London: Kegan Paul, Trench, Trübner and Co., Ltd., 1937].)

Mallon, Fr. Alexis. "Les Hébreux en Egypte," *Orientalia,* III (1921).

Maspéro, Sir Gaston. *Les Contes populaires de l'Egypte ancienne.* 4th ed.; Paris: E. Guilmoto, 1911. (Eng. trans.: *Popular Stories of Ancient Egypt,* trans. Mrs. C. H. W. Johns (A. S. Griffith) [New York: G. P. Putnam's Sons, 1915].)

————. *Histoire de l'Orient: l'Egypte, Chaldéens et Assyriens, les Israélites et les Phéniciens, les Mèdes et les Perses.* 9 vols. Paris: Hachette, 1891. (Eng. trans.: *History of Egypt, Chaldea, Syria, Babylonia and Assyria,* trans. M. L. McClure [9 vols. London: Grolier, 1901].)

Montet, Pierre. *Byblos et l'Egypte: quatre campagnes de fouilles à Gebeil, 1921-1924.* Paris: P. Geuthner, 1928.

————. *Le Drame d'Avaris: Essai sur la pénétration des Sémites en Egypte.* Paris: P. Geuthner, 1941.

————. *Les Enigmes de Tanis.* Paris: Payot, 1952.

————. *Eternal Egypt.* London: Weidenfeld and Nicolson, 1964.

————. *La géographie de l'Egypte ancienne.* 2 vols. (I. *Tomehou, la Basse-Egypte;* II. *To-chemâ, la Haute-Egypte.*) Paris: Imprimerie nationale, 1957-1961.

————. *La Nécropole royale de Tanis.* 3 vols. (I. *Les constructions et le tombeau de Osorkon II à Tanis;* II. *Les constructions et le tombeau de Psousennès à Tanis;* III. *Les constructions et le tombeau de Chéchanq III à Tanis.*) Paris: Typ. Jourde et Allard, 1947-1960.

————. *Les nouvelles fouilles de Tanis, 1929-1932.* Paris and Strasbourg: Les Belles-Lettres, 1933.

————. *Les scènes de la vie privée dans les tombeaux égyptiens de l'Ancien Empire.* Paris and Strasbourg: Librairie Istra; London and New York: H. Milford, Oxford University Press, 1925.

————. *La vie quotidienne en Egypte au temps des Ramsès.* Paris: Hachette, 1946. (Eng. trans.: *Everyday Life in Egypt in the Days of Ramesses the Great,* trans. A. R. Maxwell-Hyslop and Margaret S. Drower [London: E. Arnold; New York: St Martin's Press, 1958].)

Petrie, W. M. Flinders. *Egypt and Israel.* 2nd ed. London: Society for Promoting Christian Knowledge, 1923.

Posener, Georges. "Les Asiatiques en Egypte sous les XIIe et XIIIe dynasties," *Syria,* XXXIV (1937), 145-53.

_____. "Textes égyptiens," in *Les problèmes des Habiru à la 4e Rencontre assyriologique internationale,* ed. Jean Bottéro ("Cahiers de la Société Asiatique," 12). Paris: Imprimerie nationale, 1954.

Posener, Georges, S. Sauneron, and J. Yoyotte. *Dictionary of Egyptian Civilization.* New York: Tudor Publishing Co., 1961.

Pritchard, James B. (ed.). *Ancient Near Eastern Texts Relating to the Old Testament.* 2nd ed. Princeton: Princeton University Press, 1955.

Ranke, Hermann. *Die ägyptischen Personennamen.* 2 vols. Glückstadt: J. J. Augustin, 1935-1952.

Spiegelberg, Wilhelm. *Die ärgyptische Randglossen zum Alten Testament.* Strasbourg: Schlesier and Schweikhardt, 1906.

_____. *Der Aufenthalt Israels in Ägypten im Licht der ägyptischen Monumente.* 4th ed. Strasbourg: Schlesier und Schweikhardt, 1904.

Steindorff, Georg (ed.). *Urkunden des ägyptischen Altertums.* Leipzig: J. C. Hinrichs, 1903——

Vandier, Jacques. *La religion égyptienne.* Paris: Presses Universitaires de France, 1944.

van de Walle, Baudouin, "Hyksos," in *Dictionnaire de la Bible: Supplément,* ed. L. Pirot, A. Robert, and Henri Cazelles, Vol. IV. Paris: Letouzey et Ané, 1928——

_____. "Inscriptions égyptiennes," *ibid.,* Vol. IV.

Vergote, J. *Joseph en Egypte.* Louvain: Publications Universitaires, 1959.

Vincent, Albert. *La religion des Judéo-Araméens d'Elephantine.* Paris: P. Geuthner, 1937.

Wilson, John A. *The Burden of Egypt.* Chicago: University of Chicago Press, 1951.

_____. *The Culture of Ancient Egypt.* Chicago: University of Chicago Press, 1956. (A paperback reissue of *The Burden of Egypt.*)

Yoyotte, J. "Nechao," in *Dictionnaire de la Bible: Supplément,* ed. L. Pirot, A. Robert, and Henri Cazelles, Vol. VI. Paris: Letouzey et Ané, 1928——

_____. "Egypte ancienne," in *Histoire universelle.* Vol. I of *Encyclopédie de la Pleiade.*

Indexes

BIBLICAL REFERENCES

147

NAMES AND SUBJECTS

Index

149

Index

Index

Type, 11 on 13 and 10 on 11 Baskerville.
Display, Garamond.

DATE DUE

DEC 16 1992		
FEB 13 2003		

HIGHSMITH   #LO-45220